Popular Culture Genres

FOUNDATIONS OF POPULAR CULTURE

Series Editor: GARTH S. JOWETT
University of Houston

The study of popular culture has now become a widely accepted part of the modern academic curriculum. This increasing interest has spawned a great deal of important research in recent years, and the field of "cultural studies" in its many forms is now one of the most dynamic and exciting in modern academia. Each volume in the **Foundations of Popular Culture** series will introduce a specific issue fundamental to the study of popular culture, and the authors have been given the charge to write with clarity and precision and to examine the subject systematically. The editorial objective is to provide an important series of "building block" volumes that can stand by themselves or be used in combination to provide a thorough and accessible grounding in the field of cultural studies.

1. **The Production of Culture: Media and the Urban Arts**
   by **Diana Crane**

2. **Popular Culture Genres: Theories and Texts**
   by **Arthur Asa Berger**

3. **Rock Formation: Music, Technology, and Mass Communication**
   by **Steve Jones**

4. **Cultural Criticism: A Primer of Key Concepts**
   by **Arthur Asa Berger**

5. **Advertising and Popular Culture**
   by **Jib Fowles**

6. **Sexualities and Popular Culture**
   by **Carl B. Holmberg**

Popular Culture Genres

Theories and Texts

Arthur Asa Berger

Foundations of Popular Culture Vol. *2*

SAGE Publications
International Educational and Professional Publisher
Newbury Park   London   New Delhi

For information address:

 SAGE Publications, Inc.
2455 Teller Road
Thousand Oaks, California 91320
E-mail: order@sagepub.com

SAGE Publications Ltd.
6 Bonhill Street
London EC2A 4PU
United Kingdom

SAGE Publications India Pvt. Ltd.
M-32 Market
Greater Kailash I
New Delhi 110 048 India

Printed in the United States of America

Library of Congress Cataloging-in-Publication Data

Berger, Arthur Asa, 1933-
    Popular culture genres : theories and texts / Arthur Asa Berger.
      p. cm. — (Foundations of popular culture ; v. 2)
    Includes bibliographical references and index.
    ISBN 0-8039-4725-9 (cl.). — ISBN 0-8039-4726-7 (pb.)
    1. Mass media. 2. Popular culture. 3. Literary form. I. Title.
    II. Series.
P91.B445 1992
302.23—dc20   92-10599

99 00 01 02 03 04 10 9 8 7 6 5 4

Sage Production Editor: Astrid Virding

Contents

For Aaron and Mary Wildavsky

Series Editor's Introduction

The very essence of popular culture is its ability to provide its public with a sense of the familiar, while at the same time also infusing this with enough variety to ensure continued interest. All forms of popular culture walk the fine line between what the scholar John Cawelti (1971) has called "conventions" and "inventions." The conventions ensure that the subject matter falls into a recognizable and comfortable category, while the inventions provide the surprise (which can be either in the narrative, or in the aesthetics of presentation) which differentiates this item from the many others competing for the public's attention and money. To succeed, popular culture cannot stray too far from the recognizable formula, or categories, because the audience will experience difficulty in relating to it; but it must also constantly provide an interesting variation on the theme. It is within the context of these recognizable categories, or genres, that all of popular culture is created.

In this study, Arthur A. Berger has brought together all of the major theories relating to the nature and structure of genre. He has performed an invaluable service by explaining the significance of such important figures as Ferdinand De Saussure, Vladimir Propp, and Umberto Eco in a manner which makes the work of these philosophers accessible to readers new to the fields of popular culture studies. Also, as an aid to the reader, Berger has used a variety of figures and tables to illustrate how plot and character are structured within each genre. One of the main strengths of this book is the way in which the author develops a series of case studies of widely known texts to illustrate the various genre theories. Because the subject matter is familiar, the reader has an immediate grasp of how genre formulas work. For the student just starting in the field of popular culture studies, this book will serve as an invaluable introduction to the complex issues of narrative and structure in cultural texts.

—GARTH S. JOWETT
Series Editor

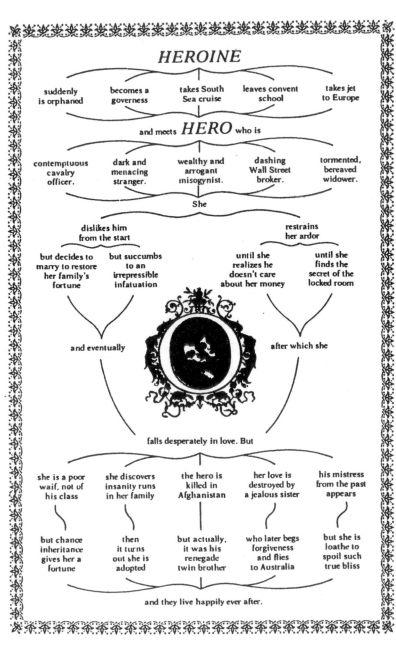

Figure 1.0. Formula for Romance novel. Reprinted with permission of the *Wilson Quarterly*.

That orthodox political history, working by custom with written documents, would tend to use arts and artifacts primarily only as illustration (when at all), is perhaps understandable, if not altogether excusable. Yet intellectual history has made hardly more use of them.

What accounts for so unnatural a state of affairs? Primarily, perhaps, the methodologies that art history has employed.

Art history has defined its data and perceived relationships between these data (arts and artifacts) and society (history) in three ways: by an aesthetic line-of-progress, as cultural expression, and by social function. These methodologies have developed successfully and cumulatively: cultural expression building on aesthetic line-of-progress, social function representing a step beyond cultural expression, not its antitheses. With social function, which considers arts and artifacts not only as aesthetic objects or reflections of the spirit of their times, but also as instruments furthering the ideological foundations of society, art history has finally become the effective and prime instrument for historical research that it should always have been, revealing and analyzing those fundamental attitudes and presuppositions by which any age lives, and on which all the institutions of every society must ultimately rest.

SOURCE: Gowans, A. (1981). *Learning to See: Historical Perspectives on Modern Popular/Commercial Arts*. Bowling Green, OH: Bowling Green University Popular Press.

Preface

This book is an introduction to the study of *genres*—a French term that means "kind" or "class." We are all conscious of genres even though we may never think much about the concept itself. For example, we talk about science fiction films or television situation comedies. Both of these terms, *science fiction* and *situation comedies*, are classifications that refer to kinds of films or television shows—that is, genres.

On the Importance of Genres

A given work, such as *The Terminator* or *Cheers* (and in the language of criticism we call them "texts") is distinctive in its own right, but it also shares certain conventions with other texts of the same genre or class. We expect certain things to happen in a science fiction film or situation comedy because we all learn the conventions of the genre as a result of watching films and television programs, reading novels, and listening to the radio. Radio stations are often genre specific; some play only country western music, others are all news, others play only soft rock, though some stations are mixed.

The study of genres is now becoming increasingly interesting to scholars who study popular culture and the mass media. There is a reason for this. We want to know how the conventions of different genres affect the creation and production of texts and the audiences of these texts. Do certain genres have social and political implications of significance? How do genres evolve? And why do some genres (such as the western) die out?

Texts and Contexts

Writing about texts (specific television shows, novels, films, etc.) without dealing with their genres is often too narrow, too focused. But writing about genres without dealing with texts that exemplify these genres is too abstract, too general. We have to deal with texts in the context of their genres to make sense of the texts themselves and the genres that shape these texts.

This book strikes a balance between the two extremes by dealing with genre theory in the first part of the book and with the analysis of classic or perhaps a better term would be *representative* texts from some of the most important genres in the second half of the book. In this section, devoted to representative texts from five important genres, I have analyzed the following works:

> *The Maltese Falcon* (tough guy detective)
> *Murder on the Orient Express* (classic detective)
> *Dr. No* (spy story)
> *War of the Worlds* (science fiction) and
> *Frankenstein* (horror)

I consider science fiction and horror to be separate genres; some critics do not. I explain the reasons for my decision in my chapter on *War of the Worlds*. All of these texts, incidently, are novels that have been made into films—and *War of the Worlds* was also made into a historic radio dramatization.

This book discusses theories relevant to understanding genres by a number of important theorists such as Vladimir Propp, Umberto

Eco, Yuri Lotman, M. M. Bakhtin, John Cawelti, Ferdinand de Saussure, Sigmund Freud, and Claude Lévi-Strauss. A great number of people have written about genres, even though there are not a large number of books devoted entirely to the subject. I also offer some notions about genres and their relation to fairy tales (which I see as a kind of prototypical genre), the kinds of heroes and heroines one finds in the different genres, and the uses and gratifications audiences obtain from the different genres, among other things.

These notions are, in some cases, speculative and should be taken as hypothetical or exploratory. This study contains an element of Freudian thought in certain places, especially in the discussions of the Oedipus complex and its relation to plot. Semiotics, the study of signs and signification, is also used, as are a number of other disciplines and techniques of analysis.

Genres, Texts, and Media

Genre studies are important because they provide us with insights about what texts are (or should be) like, how they are created, and how they function for audiences. Genres shape our expectations of what films, television shows, or videos we will be seeing or what the radio stations or songs we will be listening to will be like. Genres are also important because they enable us to talk about the relationship of texts to other texts in terms of form as well as content. The concept of intertextuality, discussed in some detail in this book, suggests that texts are often related to one another on the content level. That is, they borrow (sometimes inadvertently) from one another. But genre theory adds that texts are often related to one another on a different level, that of form—or formula.

Before the development of genre theory we were more or less limited to discussing texts, such as a spy novel like *Dr. No* and then relating these texts to the mass media, society, and culture. We might, in the case of *Dr. No*, compare and contrast the novel and the film that was made from it. There was a gigantic leap we had to make, from a specific text to the mass media. Now, with the recognition of the importance of genres, we have an intermediary step—one that enlarges and enhances our understanding of the way texts function and of the way that texts relate to one another, the media, and society.

In the past, it could be argued, we have dealt with genres in a more or less cursory manner, mentioning genres here and there in books of criticism, but not devoting the sustained analysis of genres, in general, that they warrant. On the other hand, we have also produced a number of works on specific genres and dealt with genre theory in passing, so to speak, in these books. In recent years, fortunately, we have become more interested in genre theory and have been investigating it on a more sustained basis.

A Historical View of the Study of Genres

Genre studies can be said to have started with Aristotle (384-322 B.C.) and his book on poetics. The first sentence of *De Poetica* *(Poetics)* suggests the importance of genres.

> Our subject being Poetry, I propose to speak not only of the art in general but also of its species and their respective capacities. . . . Epic poetry and Tragedy, as also Comedy . . . are all, viewed as a whole, modes of imitation.

Aristotle is interested in the various kinds of poems (and plays) and suggests that these are tragedy, epic poetry, and comedy.

Comedy, he adds, is "an imitations of men worse than average" (in terms of being ridiculous, that is) while tragedy is "essentially an imitation not of persons but of action and life, of happiness and misery." Aristotle's distinctions between comedy and tragedy and epic show that he was classifying works according to certain things they had in common. It is this notion, that individual works—films, television programs, novels, and other kinds of artistic creations—may be distinctive in certain respects but are related to other works—that is the subject of the first part of this book.

Speculation about genres and their importance is not confined to those who study the popular arts and mass media. Literary theorists have also been interested in the nature of genre for many years. Northrop Frye, a Canadian professor, wrote *Anatomy of Criticism* in 1957, an influential book that deals with genres and literature.

For our purposes, however, we can say that in the United States, the study of genres in the mass media started gaining momentum about forty years ago. Robert Warshow published a book of previously written essays, *The Immediate Experience: Movies, Comics, Theatre and Other Aspects of Popular Culture*, that contained two important chapters—one on gangster films and the other on westerns (and, of interest also, an essay on horror comics) that might be recognized as genre criticism. The book appeared in 1962, but the essay on gangster films originally appeared in 1948 and the essay on westerns appeared in 1954.

In 1970, Jim Kitses published *Horizons West*, an important book on "Authorship within the Western." The first chapter, "Authorship and Genre: Notes on the Western" explicitly raises the problem of an "American tradition" and its impact on three important directors of westerns. Kitses wanted to avoid focusing on directors (auteurs) and "the cult of personality." As he writes:

> In place of the reactionary notion that Hollywood directors function like the charismatic heroes of their films, I have wanted to advance the idea of an American *tradition*, of which the western seems to me an admirable and central model.

In this chapter Kitses offers a chart listing oppositions between the individual and the community, nature and culture, and the West and the East that, he suggests, are found in westerns.

The publication of John Cawelti's *The Six-Gun Mystique* in 1971 was a major event in genre criticism. In this book (which I discuss in some detail in my chapters on genre theory) Cawelti used a number of different perspectives to make sense of the western— psychoanalytic theory, Marxist theory, and historical analysis, among others. This brief book is concerned primarily with the western but it also has implications for all kinds of genre studies and the relation of genres and formulas.

In 1974, Stuart M. Kaminsky, a professor of film at Northwestern University, published *American Film Genres: Approaches to a Critical Theory of Popular Film*. This book had chapters on topics such as westerns (which it compared with Samurai films), gangster films, horror films, science fiction films, comedies, and the work of two important "Genre Directors"—Donald Siegal and John Ford.

About this time, in 1976, I published *The TV-Guided American*, which was a study of a number of important television shows of that period. In the book I selected programs that were representative of the various genres, to which I alluded in the Introduction:

> Strictly speaking, it is not television per se, as a medium, but certain kinds of programs, sports programs, advertisements, situation comedies, space operas, detective and crime adventures, westerns, a whole world (or wasteland) of all kinds of different programs that we subsume under the general term "television." (p. 9)

In the book I chose programs that I considered to be interesting and representative of the major genres—to analyze. The book also has two chapters that deal with English television, but these chapters are not focused on genres.

Stuart Kaminsky followed up his book on film genres with a book on television genres. *American Television Genres*, published in 1986 (with Jeffrey H. Mahan and a number of other collaborators), is somewhat different in structure from the film book. *American Television Genres* is concerned with genres, but it uses a number of different methodologies of interpretation in dealing with genres: historical and structural approaches, psychological approaches, and sociological and anthropological approaches are covered. There are chapters that use the ideas of thinkers such as Northrop Frye, Carl Jung, Erik Erikson, and Sigmund Freud.

A recent book by Tim Bywater and Thomas Sobchack, *An Introduction to Film Criticism: Major Critical Approaches to Narrative Film*, appeared in 1989. It contained an excellent chapter on genre criticism that has a brief summary of its development as well as some interesting philosophical questions about this form of criticism. For example, they point out that critics tend to assume that genres exist and do not as a rule spend too much energy justifying their assumption. They write that

> essentially the problem is the question of which came first, the chicken or the egg. One has to select a group of films prior to identifying them as a genre; however, the very selection is shaped by a definition of the genre supposedly not yet arrived at. What makes a critic talk about musicals as a group is some prior notion of what a musical is.
>
> Initial attempts to identify genres emphasized the obvious similarities among films: themes, configurations of action (private-eye's pursuit of truth), subject matter (cowboys), objects and costumes (machine guns and dapper suits in films about the underworld). It is therefore not surprising that the largest body of generic criticism has been about film groups with the most viable characteristics: the western, the gangster film, the hard-boiled detective film, and the traditional horror film. These genres take place in specific settings and in certain time-frames, they have clearly identifiable plots, conventions and characters, and the are full of visually obvious and repeatedly used objects, the latter becoming iconic (the white hat on the good cowboy) in their ability to convey thematic and dramatic information beyond their material function and presence in a single film. (p. 90)

Bywater and Sobchack raise an important philosophical question about the nature of classification and reality—one that is dealt with in Chapter 1.

The last item in this brief (and selective) bibliographical survey of genre criticism is Leah R. Vande Berg and Lawrence A. Wenner's anthology, *Television Criticism: Approaches and Applications* (1991). Although this book is not exclusively devoted to genre criticism, a considerable number of the essays in the book make use of genre theory. This suggests that genre criticism is now seen as an established and important method of criticism, a technique that must be taken into consideration whenever a text is interpreted.

I hope that in writing a book that deals with both genre theory and with the analysis of significant texts in five of the most important genres, *Popular Culture Genres: Theories and Texts* will provide useful insights about genres and their importance for media analysts and critics. I also hope that the analysis of significant texts that I have done will help readers gain some insights about how they can make their own analyses of specific texts and relate these texts to their genres, to the mass media, to society and culture.

Acknowledgments

This book is part of a series of studies of popular culture edited by Garth Jowett, and I would like to thank him for his encouragement and for the many useful suggestions he made about the manuscript. It has benefitted greatly from the careful reading he gave it in a preliminary version. I also am grateful to Ann West, my editor at Sage Publications, for her support on this project and on a number of others, as well. Since she came to Sage Publications, my fortunes have improved considerably.

I appreciate permission granted by the *Wilson Quarterly* to use the chart, "Formula for Romance Novels"; permission granted by Larry Tritten to use his clever chart, "The Country Western Song Plot Formulator," and his extremely witty chart "Make Your Own James Bond Movie."

I also was aided by the efforts of many scholars, writers, and philosophers—from Aristotle to Umberto Eco—whose works on genres and related concerns are used in the book. Critics of my work usually fall into two camps. One camp argues my work is "far out and ridiculous" and the other camp argues that "everyone knows this stuff already." Whether *Popular Culture Genres* is one or the other, both, or somewhere in between, is something readers will have to decide for themselves.

PART I

Theories

Genre study in film is based on the realization that certain popular narrative forms have both cultural and universal roots, that the Western of today is related to archetypes of the past 200 years in the United States and to the folk tale and the myth. A major value in examining particular genres of film is in discovering what elements we are responding to. An examination of what in a form makes it popular, makes it survive, relates it to forms that exist before it, informs us about what there is in film to which we respond.

The argument that people go to films simply for entertainment is fine, as far as it goes, but it does not answer the questions of why certain forms persist, why others rise and fade, why a man responds to detective stories and not to romances, why one society's dominant form is violent and another's passive. In essence, what is the nature of the entertainment that one is responding to?

SOURCE: Kaminsky, S. M. (1974, p. 3). *American Film Genres*. Dayton, OH: Pflaum Publishing.

1

On the Structure of Genres

On the Nature of Genres

There is a considerable amount of controversy among literary and communication scholars about what a genre is and what importance genres have in the scheme of things. For our purposes I equate a genre with a kind or type of radio program, television program, or film and not with forms such as comedy, tragedy, or epic (which is the way many literary scholars have dealt with genres). An examination of the television listings in any newspaper will reveal a large number of programs that can be subsumed under a much smaller number of genres.

The most important television genres are: commercials, news shows, documentaries, situation comedies, soap operas, talk shows, interview shows, science shows, game shows, sports programs (football, baseball, basketball, track, etc.), action-adventure police shows (once it would have been westerns), science fiction shows, how-to shows (cooking, fixing houses), and so forth. Many of these genres have subgenres, too.

The word *genre* is French and means "kind" (or gender) and is very similar to our term *generic*. One buys generic peas or beans in cans which do not have brand names and saves money, generally speaking, by not paying for advertising.

When we decide to watch a television show we usually consider, among other things, the kind of program we will be watching. Is it a situation comedy or an action-adventure show or a soap? We know, in general terms, what to expect from each kind of program or, more precisely, what kind of gratifications we might expect from each genre. That is because we know what these shows are like, though we may not know what a particular episode of a show will deal with. I will deal with program types shortly and offer some ideas about how we might deal with them, but before doing this I would like to briefly discuss a philosophical program related to the matter of genres.

A Philosophical Footnote

A genre, let us recall, is a class of programs. There is a class we call situation-comedies and a particular episode of *Cheers* is a member of this class. The philosophers have raised an interesting question related to all this—namely, do classes exist? Let me quote from *Philosophy: An Introduction* by John Herman Randall, Jr. and Justus Buchler (1962) on the argument between nominalists (*nomen* is Latin for name) and realists.

> Since earliest times philosophers have differed over how the furniture of the universe, so to speak, should be interpreted. Some have felt that only *particular things* should be called "real." Others have felt that *kinds* of things are not less real than this or that thing. In the later Middle Ages, when this controversy was at its height, it took the form of a dispute as to whether "universals" are as real as particulars. By a "universal" is to be understood what is represented by terms like "white*ness*," "triangu*larity*," "father*hood*" . . . by a "particular" we mean what is represented by terms like "*that* white chair," "*the* triangle *just drawn on the board*." Those who denied the reality of universals were called *nominalists*, those who affirmed it *realists*. According to the realists, universals are qualities *common* to a group of particular things. The qualities which things have in common, they maintained, are no less qualities than the qualities which each of the things has individually. (p. 192)

The nominalists countered this argument by asking how something that does not exist (a class of programs, for example) can be called real?

The argument, our authors tell us, can be broached in broader terms. It boils down to whether nature can be described only in terms of specific things and of facts or whether relations and laws about nature are real. "Are relations and laws mere fictions, verbal conveniences?" our authors ask (p. 193).

Aristotle had a solution (generally known as *conceptualism*) that is of relevance to our interest in genres and specific programs. He avoided either position by suggesting that every object in nature has two aspects—matter and form. Thus anything has both specificity, distinctiveness, individuality, concreteness on one hand and form, character, generality on the other. The first aspect, which we can *sense*, tells us that something exists, that it is; the second aspect, which we can *know*, tells us what something is.

I have a dog named *Patches*. She is an individual dog, has a particular life history, and so forth. But she also is a member of a general class of animals, dogs, and a subcategory, Cockapoos. Can we only talk about this dog or that dog without talking about dogs in general? Or does the concept "dog" have a reality to it? If you have a philosophic mind and are interested in pursuing this problem, most introduction to philosophy textbooks deal with it in some detail.

Television Program Types

The question I set out to solve in my analysis of television genres is whether there are ways of reducing the wide variety of television genres to something more fundamental, more basic. After considering a number of possibilities, I concluded that for all practical purposes, all of the important television genres can be reduced to four types of programs. These are:

1. *Actualities,*
2. *Contests,*

3. *Persuasions,* and
4. *Dramas.*

Let me explain how these particular terms are being used. *Actualities* are programs, such as a news show or documentary, in which the emphasis is on portraying what is going on in the world (as contrasted to making things up, inventing a world of one's own). I realize there is an interpretative aspect to news shows and documentaries, but at least they are focused on actual events, people, and so forth in society.

Contests refer to programs in which there is some kind of real competition, programs that are not dramatic fictions. Contests have players, not actresses and actors—at least when the contests are legitimate. The dominant television contests are sports programs and game shows.

Persuasions are programs meant to convince people to do something or believe something. Persuasion involves getting people to believe something by argument and entreaty that affects their beliefs and actions. Commercials are the dominant form of television persuasions. Because there are so many different kinds of commercials, some of which employ dramatic sequences, it is difficult to deal with commercials except in terms of their intent, which I have taken as basic.

Dramas are one of the most important forms on television and in all media. I consider programs such as soap operas, situation comedies, police shows, action-adventure shows, hospital shows, and so forth as dramas. Their common characteristics are that they are all narrative fictions in which there is conflict of either a serious or comic nature. Sports shows are often dramatic, but that is because the outcome is not clear; but sports programs are not fictions.

These four types of programs can, in turn, be subsumed under an even more basic set of concepts—concepts that help us categorize each of the four types of programs in various ways.

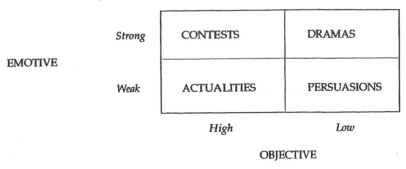

	Strong	CONTESTS	DRAMAS
EMOTIVE	Weak	ACTUALITIES	PERSUASIONS

	High	Low

OBJECTIVE

Figure 1.1. Objective-Emotive aspects of television texts.

The Emotive-Objective Polarity

There are, I would suggest, a set of polar oppositions that explain or explicate important elements in all program types and genres. These polar opposites can be labeled the *objective* and the *emotive*. By objective I mean that which expresses the nature of reality as it is, or as we can know it. The "objective" is the world of things, the world of events that actually happen (as contrasted to fictions that involve make-believe events that never really happened), the world of the rational (which might be a better term?).

The emotive, on the other hand, involves the affective aspects of consciousness—personal feelings, emotions, that sort of thing.

It is possible to set up a four-celled figure (Figure 1.1) that uses the objective-emotive polarity to explicate my four program types and give us some insights into the various genres that fall under each program type.

Let me use this diagram to discuss some important genres. Sports programs are classified as contests and are high under objective (because they actually exist) and strong under emotive, in that they generate a great deal of excitement in viewers (unless the game is dull, that is). News programs would be high under objective and should be weak under emotive, though stations with local news shows that emphasize killings, rapes, drug busts, and

TABLE 1.1 Television Genres and the Emotive-Objective Polarities

Genre	Emotive	Objective
News	Weak	High
Sports	Strong	High
Sitcoms	Strong	Low
Commercials	Weak	Low
Documentaries	Weak	High
Soaps	Strong	Low
Police	Strong	Low
Game Shows	Strong	High
Spectacles	Strong	High
Talk Shows	Weak	High

so forth are not. Editorials would be classified as persuasions, not actualities.

Dramas, of course, would be low on the objective scale but strong on the emotive one. They are fictions meant to generate feelings in viewers. Persuasions would be low on the objective scale and weak on the emotive scale. This is somewhat problematical in that many commercials are dramatic, exciting, and so forth. But if we take persuasions at face value, in the most literal sense, they attempt to convince us to do something and should be weak on emotion or affect. The table above lists some of the more important television genres and shows how they rate in terms of the emotive-objective polarity.

Using the objective-emotive polarity it is possible to gain a better understanding of the nature of the various genres and their appeals. A content analysis of the most popular genres on television would indicate that dramas are exceedingly important and, therefore, that programs which are strong on the emotive side and low on the objective side tend to dominate. Television programming tends to be dramatic and even genres that are not explicitly dramatic, such as news shows and commercials, often have a great deal of dramatic content to them.

On the Importance of the
Dramatic on TV

The importance of drama to television is discussed by Martin Esslin (1982) in *The Age of Television* when he writes that

> the language of television is none other than that of *drama*; that television—as indeed the cinema, with which it has much in common—is, in its essence, *a dramatic medium*; and that looking at TV from the point of view and with the analytic tools of dramatic criticism and theory might contribute to a better understanding of its nature and many aspects of its psychological, social, and cultural impact, both in the short term and on a long term, macroscopic time scale. (pp. 6, 7)

When you consider the amount of time the typical American spends watching television, you come up with an interesting statistic. "*The average American adult sees the equivalent of five to six full-length stage plays a week!*" (Esslin, 1982, p. 7). In addition to this, I would add that much of what is shown on television (aside from narratives) has a dramatic content, also.

The fact of the matter is that although technology is opening up new methods of carrying programs, there are still only a limited number of genres or formats that are available to us—so new channels often focus on a particular kind of program (all MTV, all humor, all news). There has not been very much new under the sun when it comes to genre development, so new technologies, cable, satellites, and so forth are stuck with the same old kinds of programs and the same old formulas. The only variations involve the mix of genres or the stylistic innovations individual directors may bring to their work or, in some cases, the mixing of genres in one program (*Twin Peaks*, for example, mixed the seriality of the soap opera with horror).

It may be worthwhile thinking about what impact this diet of drama has for the American public. If we see too much drama, especially if it is violent (as much television drama tends to be) we may become desensitized and, if we are exposed to certain kinds of drama at too young an age, suffer from anxieties about growing up and having relationships with others and various other afflictions.

There is also the problem of why certain dramatic forms become popular and why some die out (the Western, for instance). There may be an element of overkill in such cases and it also may be that the dominant values expressed in Westerns lose their meaning and do not resonate with the values of the public. This matter and the question of what exposure to dramatic genres may be doing to us will be discussed in more detail shortly.

The popularity of a pseudo-sport or hybrid such as wrestling on television is a phenomenon worth investigating—as is the rebirth of the situation comedy and the decline of science fiction programs on television—but not on film.

Relationships Among Genres

In Figure 1.1 we find that diagonals are the most distant program types. Thus actualities and dramas, contests and persuasions are the furthest removed from one another. This is because the diagonal cells do not share either the objectivity of the horizontal axis or the emotiveness of the vertical axis. Actualities, for instance, are "weak-high" in the emotive-objective scale while dramas are "strong-low" on that scale.

Actualities and contests, in the same manner, are high on the objective scale and dramas and persuasions are low on this measure. Please remember that I am using *objective* in a special way: to deal with real life and real events, in contrast to dramatic recreations of life or narrative fictions.

What complicates matters is that several overlaps are caused by the creation of new mixed genres, such as the docudrama, and the fact that at times all four program types can get mixed together (as in some commercials). What my schema does is enable us to see what each genre is supposed to be like. If we find, for example, that television news programs are strong on the emotive (as they frequently are) instead of being strong on the objective, we have reason to wonder what is going on and whether the news departments are betraying the trust we put in them. And dramas that fail to move us because they are too high on the objective side and too weak on the emotive side are obviously deficient.

I have offered a guide to the structure of genres, specifically using television as an example, but these concepts can equally be used to study the genre forms on other media. It may be that the most interesting and successful shows on television are the ones that transcend their boundaries (though, as I pointed out with news, there are dangers involved, as well). I would hope that my schema will help us understand something about the nature of genres and their components, and will be useful when we wish to interpret and analyze them.

The story should be 192 pages in length—50,000 to 56,000 words. There is to be no violence in those pages, no blood, no pain and certainly no "slangy, obscene or profane" language. Love scenes in bed are permitted only if the Hero and the Heroine are married.

The Heroine, like the rest of the characters, is a curious composite of qualities rated highly by romance readers. She is anywhere between 19 and 27 years old—presumably the ideal age as far as the readers are concerned. She is a virgin and neither drinks nor smokes. Unlike the Other Woman, who is always "mean, oversophisticated and well-groomed," the Heroine "is not beautiful in the high fashion sense and wears modest makeup and clothes," although "her outfits are described in detail, as is her physical appearance."

The Hero is 8 to 12 years older than the Heroine, and while "he is not necessarily handsome, he is virile." "He is never married to anyone but our heroine," read the instructions, "but may be widowed, and even divorced, provided it is made clear that his ex-wife sought the divorce."

SOURCE: Kakutani, M. (1980, September 7). "Exotic packaged romances of happiness always and forever." *This World Magazine, San Francisco Chronicle.*

2

Propp, de Saussure, and the Narrative

Narratives, it was suggested in Chapter 1, are one of the dominant genres found on television and in the media in general. But what exactly is a narrative or story (or in the language used in this book, a *drama*) and how do narratives work? This is a problem that has puzzled critics and literary theorists since Aristotle's time and there are many books on the subject—books that tend to be highly technical and rather esoteric. There is a scholar whose contributions are both enormously important and highly accessible, a Russian folklorist named Vladimir Propp, whose theories will now be considered. In the discussion that follows, Propp's theories will be connected to those of the Swiss linguist Ferdinand de Saussure to provide us with a means of analyzing narratives and understanding how they work. I will also provide a case study in which Propp's concepts will be used to analyze an important James Bond novel, *Dr. No*.

Propp on the Folktale

Vladimir Propp's *Morphology of the Folktale* (Propp, 1968) is generally acknowledged to be one of the most important contributions to our understanding of narratives. Though written in 1928 and

13

devoted to analyzing a collection of Russian folktales, it still remains useful and offers important insights for those interested in narrative theory and related matters—such as the nature of formulas, the role of heroes and heroines in stories, and so on. That is because it has wide applicability to all kinds of narratives in all kinds of genres—such as detective stories, spy stories, action-adventure stories, and science fiction stories.

As Alan Dundes (Propp, 1968) writes in the introduction to Propp's book:

> Propp's analysis should be useful in analyzing the structure of literary forms (such as novels and plays), comic strips, motion picture and television plots, and the like. In understanding the interrelationship between folklore and literature, and between folklore and the mass media, the emphasis has hitherto been principally on content. Propp's *Morphology* suggests that there can be structural borrowings as well as content borrowings. (pp. xiv, xv)

What Propp did was elicit 31 "functions," which he described as *"an act of a character, defined from the point of view of its significance for the course of the action."* He added to this that the functions of characters *"serve as stable, constant elements in a tale, independent of how and by whom they are fulfilled"* and also that there are a limited number of functions found in fairy tales.

He dismisses classifying fairy tales according to categories or themes because, he suggests, nobody has come up with an acceptable method of determining what categories or themes are to be used. Every author, he says, defines themes his own way and creates his own system of analysis, generally without a consistent principle of division. If neither categories of folktales or themes found in folktales (and by extension other narratives) are useful, the functions of characters are, he suggests. Propp moved from the plane of content (themes, etc.) to that of form and structure (functions of characters), which is why he used the term *morphology* in his title.

His book deals with the syntagmatic or sequential development of a story, as heroes are sent on missions, fight with villains, fall in love with and marry princesses, and so on. This syntagmatic analysis is often contrasted with a methodology espoused by the French anthropologist Claude Lévi-Strauss: a *paradigmatic* analysis that looks for the patterns of oppositions hidden in texts and tells us what texts "mean" rather than what happens in texts, as Propp's method does.

His list of 31 functions (which come after the initial situation) follows—in a highly abbreviated format (Table 2.1).

I should point out that for Propp there are two kinds of heroes: *seeker heroes*, those who seek something, are sent off on some task, and so forth and *victimized heroes*, those who must leave home to fight against villains, but are not sent specifically to seek something. In any one tale, Propp tells us, there is either a seeker hero or a victimized hero; never both. The victimized hero (who always leaves home) may have adventures but he is not specifically seeking something, such as trying to find a kidnapped princess.

Sample Propp Function

Propp's functions often involve a number of different actions that may occur. To show this, consider one of the functions, mediation. Propp describes this function as follows:

IX. MISFORTUNE OR LACK IS MADE KNOWN; THE HERO IS APPROACHED WITH A REQUEST OR COMMAND; HE IS ALLOWED TO GO OR HE IS DISPATCHED. (Definition: *mediation, the connective incidents.* Designation: B.) (1968, p. 36)

Propp then lists seven different varieties of mediation:

1. *A call for help is given, with the resultant dispatch of the hero* (B1).
2. *The hero is dispatched directly* (B2).
3. *The hero is allowed to depart from home* (B3).
4. *Misfortune is announced* (B4).
5. *The banished hero is transported away from home* (B5).
6. *The hero condemned to death is secretly freed* (B6)
7. *A lament is sung* (B7).

TABLE 2.1 Propp's 31 Functions of Characters

Function			Description of Function
	α	Initial Situation	Members of family introduced, Hero introduced
1.	β	Absentation	One of the members of the family absents self
2.	γ	Interdiction	Interdiction addressed to hero (Can be reversed)
3.	δ	Violation	Interdiction is violated
4.	E	Reconnaissance	The villain makes attempt to get information
5.	ζ	Delivery	The villain gets information about his victim
6.	η	Trickery	The villain tries to deceive his victim
7.	θ	Complicity	Victim is deceived
8.	A	Villainy	Villain causes harm to a member of a family, or
		Lack	Member of family lacks something, desires something
9.	B	Mediation	Misfortune made known. Hero dispatched
10.	C	Counteraction	Hero (Seeker) agrees to, decides on counteraction
11.	↑	Departure	Hero leaves home
12.	D	1st Donor Function	Hero tested, receives magical agent or helper
13.	E	Hero's Reaction	Hero reacts to agent or donor
14.	F	Receipt of Agent	Hero acquires use of magical agent
15.	G	Spacial Change	Hero led to object of search
16.	H	Struggle	Hero and villain join in direct combat
17.	J	Branding	Hero is branded
18.	I	Victory	Villain is defeated
19.	K	Liquidation	Initial misfortune or lack is liquidated
20.	↓	Return	Hero returns
21.	Pr	Pursuit, Chase	Hero is pursued
22.	Rs	Rescue	Hero rescued from pursuit
23.	O	Unrec. Arrival	Hero, unrecognized, arrives home or elsewhere
24.	L	Unfounded Claims	False hero presents unfounded claims
25.	M	Difficult Task	Difficult task is proposed to hero
26.	N	Solution	The task is resolved
27.	R	Recognition	The hero is recognized
28.	Ex	Exposure	The false hero or villain is exposed
29.	T	Transfiguration	The hero is given a new appearance
30.	U	Punishment	The villain is punished
31.	W	Wedding	The hero is married, ascends the throne

Each of these variations is described in some detail, so that Propp's discussion of this one function takes several pages. His discussion of the function in which the hero acquires a magical agent takes more than seven pages. Some other functions only involve a few sentences, however. The point, then, is that many of the functions listed in the table generally have a number of variations and some functions are more important than others. Some functions can be reversed and others can be interpreted implicitly, so things can get complicated.

A Variation on Propp

In this variation I will adopt some of the functions and characters used by Propp and apply them using an insight from Ferdinand de Saussure, one of the founding fathers of semiology. His great insight was that meaning is based on relationships. As he wrote in his *Course in General Linguistics,* "concepts are purely differential and defined not by their positive content but negatively by their relations with the other terms of the system." The most important aspect of concepts is, he added, "in being what the others are not" (1966, p. 117). The most important relationship, for our purposes, is that of polar oppositions. In Table 2.2 a number of Propp's functions and characters are placed in a system of polar oppositions.

Table 2.2 begins with the basic oppositions found in many narratives—a hero in some kind of conflict with a villain. Propp suggests, remember, that there are two kinds of heroes: victim heroes, who suffer from the actions of a villain and seeker heroes, who must "leave home" on some kind of a quest. Propp's analysis of his Russian fairy tales lead him to a definition of heroes. He writes that

> the hero of a fairy tale is that character who either directly suffers from the action of the villain . . . or who agrees to liquidate the misfortune or lack of another person. In the course of the action the hero is the person who is supplied with a magical agent (a magical helper), and who makes use of it or is served by it.

TABLE 2.2 Polarities in Proppian Functions

Heroic	Villainous
Hero seeks something or suffers from villains acts	Villain hinders seeker hero or punishes hero
Undergoes ordeals	Makes hero undergo ordeals
Is dispatched	Engages in reconnaissance
Gets helpers (magic powers)	Has henchmen (evil skills)
Heroines (rescued)	Enchantresses (bewitch heroes)
Seeming villainesses shown good	False heroes shown bad
Love	Lust
Young (sons)	Old (fathers)
Handsome	Ugly, often grotesque
Individualist	Collectivist
Righteous warrior	Evil kingdom
Imagination, invention	Technology, force
Finds donor figures	Hinders donor figures
Obtains magic agents, helpers	Hinders magic agents, helpers
Defeats villain	Loses to hero

In the case of suffering directly from the actions of a villain, the situation is relatively simple. But even on quests, to liquidate misfortunes or take care of some lack by others, the hero confronts some kind of villain. So the hero is always in conflict with a villain.

Opposing Actions or Functions

In Table 2.3, which follows, I offer some of the more common acts of characters or what Propp would call *functions* in terms of polar oppositions. These functions are, as Propp argued, the building blocks out of which narratives are constructed and represent an action by one character and a reaction or counteraction by an opposing character.

These actions and characters are, for the most part, taken from Propp but put into bipolar relationships so that their function is clear. What I have done, I suggest, is to make explicit what is implicit. That is, every time we think of a villain, we must think of

TABLE 2.3 Actions, Goals, and Characters in Narratives

Basic Actions of Characters			
Cooperate	Compete	Search for	Evade
Help	Hinder	Tell Truth	Lie
Escape	Imprison	Allow	Prohibit
Defend	Attack	Question	Answer
Initiate	Respond	Rescue	Endanger
Disguise	Uncover	Protect	Threaten
Pretend	Reveal	Suffer	Punish
Love	Hate	Dispatch	Summon
Unravel	Mystify	Allow	Interdict
Pursue	Evade	Retain	Lose

Goals of Heroes	Goals of Villains
Overcome a villain	Overcome a hero
Rescue a victim	Kidnap a victim
Succeed in a quest or task	Prevent hero from quest or task
Make up for a lack	Create a lack
Freedom	Enslavement

Primary Characters	
Heroes	Villains
Aides	Henchmen
Princesses	Sirens
Magicians	Sorcerers
Donors	Preventers
Dispatchers	Retrievers
Seekers	Avoiders
Seeming villains	False heroes/heroines
Rulers	Commoners

a hero (or if we think of a villainess we must think of a heroine) because concepts gain their meaning by relationships. In the same sense, every time we follow some action by some character, we interpret this action in terms of counteractions by opposing characters.

Heroes and Villains

Propp noticed that heroes have helpers of one sort or another—people, animals, magic weapons (sometimes all three)—and these helpers support the hero in his fight with the villain and enable the hero to triumph. Villains, of course, have their helpers, too—what I have called *henchmen*, taking advantage of the negative associations connected with that term—who represent the other side of the equation.

One of the traditional tasks of the hero is to help heroines who are in trouble or rescue them from villains (or both). In modern narratives it is possible to have powerful heroines, and we occasionally find them, but generally speaking it is still the heroes who are strong and active while the heroines remain weak and passive. This is changing somewhat. A figure such as Princess Leia in *Star Wars* is a case in point, as are the characters in *Thelma and Louise*.

The hero-villain conflict is, indirectly, a conflict between good and evil; we know that good will win, generally speaking, but it is seeing *how* good wins that interests us. Connected to the notion of goodness is that of freedom. Heroes and their helpers fight for freedom. In some cases this means escaping from an evil empire (as was the case in the "Death Star" episode in *Star Wars*), but it also involves neutralizing the power of the villain and his followers and, if possible, destroying the evil empire.

One of the basic motivations of heroes, who tend to be young, is that of romantic love—of the hero for the heroine. Countering that is the lust of the villains, who tend to be old. Obviously, a conflict between a young male and an old villain over a woman has Oedipal aspects to it that need to be considered. We might ask ourselves whether heroes are, in some way, connected to the "battle" we fought when we were young (so Freud suggests) with an older "villain," for the love of a beautiful woman—our mothers. Is there an element of repetition compulsion here and a need to triumph, if only in fantasy, a means of assuaging the traumatic defeat we suffered at an earlier age?

In the classic confrontations, a righteous warrior (perhaps armed with magical agents and assisted by powerful helpers, as was Luke

Skywalker in *Return of the Jedi* when he had the power of "the force") confronts an older, evil villain, who has an evil empire at his command (and in the film, curiously, turns out to be Luke's father). There is a kind of individualist-collectivist aspect to these confrontations in which the figures represent freedom and totalitarianism, goodness and evil.

The righteous hero has courage, imagination, inventiveness, and a number of magic agents and helpers, supplied usually by a donor figure. With these qualities and powers the hero is able to defeat the villain and his superior numbers, generally after having undergone ordeals. In the case of *Star Wars*, the donor figures are the Jedi knights who impart their knowledge to Luke. He also has his magical light saber. In *Return of the Jedi* the Ewoks function as magic helpers. Without them, Luke and his friends could never have defeated the evil empire.

One moral we derive from all this is that the hero cannot function effectively all on his own, though the degree to which heroes are alone varies considerably. The hero generally needs others and though he fights for freedom and justice, and individual rights, these terms are shown to be connected to some kind of good society. Heroes traditionally are not asocial or antisocial. Villains, on the other hand, tend to be alienated and unloved and they sublimate their sexual longings and aberrations into a quest for power and domination. Villains may have enchantresses who work with them, or captive women, and have sexual relations with them, but generally speaking women (or at least normal women) do not love villains, though they may be intoxicated by their wealth and power.

Fairy Tales and Modern Tales

What I have been arguing is that modern popular culture genres can be thought of as involving variations, modifications, camouflaged versions, and so forth of what Propp called fairy tales. A large number of the functions that Propp found in his Russian fairy tales can also be found in contemporary spy stories, science fiction stories, soap operas, westerns, and the like. This is probably because what Propp did, really, was discover some of the basic functions found in all narratives, even though he was investigating one particular kind—the fairy tale.

I have modified Propp in an effort to make him more accessible and easier to understand and tried to suggest how his notions can help us understand narratives better—especially in their modern manifestations. There are of course differences; we cannot interpret Propp's functions too literally. (Thus, when he writes that the hero marries the princess we can update and modernize this concept and say that in many modern tales, the hero has sex with some woman who he has rescued from a villain or helped in some way.) Nor must we assume that the functions will always occur in a particular order, as Propp did.

What we learn from Propp is that there is a logic to narratives and that they are constructed according to rules that have not varied greatly over the centuries. There are heroes and heroines, there are villains and villainesses, there is conflict, there are helpers, there are magic agents or powers that the heroes have and that the villains have, and so on. Heroes, whether they are knights, cowboys, soldiers, robots, androids, or cyborgs do certain kinds of things (such as rescue damsels in distress and thwart the heinous plans of evil and ruthless villains) and have done these things since we started telling stories. When we add Saussure's (1966) insight about concepts to Propp we learn that all figures in narratives (and all their actions) have meaning because of other figures who oppose them (and oppose their actions) in one way or another. What makes stories exciting is conflict—but as Propp showed us, there are different kinds of conflict and various kinds of actions by the characters to be considered. The battle between the hero and the villain is just the tip of the narrative iceberg.

Dr. No—A Case Study

Let me offer a synopsis of Ian Fleming's spy novel, Dr. No—a book that is typical of the genre and a book about one of the most popular heroes of recent years.

The story starts out with two British spies in Jamaica, John Strangeways and Mary Trueblood, being killed by mysterious half-breed Chinese-Negroes (Chigroes) and dumped into the Caribbean in a weighted coffin. James Bond, agent 007 (licensed to kill) is summoned by M, the chief of the British espionage organization, and told to investigate the disappearance. Bond had been injured in a previous assignment and M thinks sending Bond to Jamaica would be something of a rest cure. But before Bond is sent off, M insists that the armorer supply Bond with a new weapon, replacing the Beretta Bond had used for many years, which had got stuck in a crucial situation. The armorer, Major Boothroyd, chooses a Walther PPK 7.65mm gun and a Berns Martin triple-draw holster for Bond. Bond is sent to Jamaica where various attempts are made on his life: he is sent poisoned fruit, a centipede is left in his room, and so forth. He secures the assistance an old friend, a black man, Quarrel, who helps Bond get back in shape. Together they investigate a mysterious island that has attracted their attention. This is an island owned by a mysterious figure, Dr. Julius No, a six-foot-six half-German, half-Chinese madman with metal claws instead of hands who schemes to take control of the world. When Bond and Quarrel sneak onto the island they discover a blonde goddess (with a disfigured nose)—a beautiful nature girl named Honeychile Rider. She has come to the island to search for shells. Dr. No sends out a crew in a strange mechanical contraption that resembles a dragon. His men kill Quarrel and capture Bond and Honeychile. No owns the island, which seems only to be a nesting place for birds that produce guano (bird feces) and which is run by slavelike Chigroes. They work deep in the bowels of the island fortress. From his island, Dr. No monitors and destroys American missiles (for which he is rewarded by the Russians). Bond is imprisoned in a room where he can live indefinitely, as a prisoner, or try to escape by making his way through a long shaft leading to the sea that has various features designed to kill him and ends up subjecting him to varying ordeals. Honeychile is set out on the sand, tied to stakes, to be eaten by crabs. Bond has only a cigarette lighter, a knife (which he stole when having dinner with Dr. No) as weapons. He also fashions a weapon from the ventilation grill over the shaft. Bond

TABLE 2.4 Proppian Functions of *Dr. No*

Proppian Functions	Symbol	Events in the Text
Initial situation	α	Agents introduced in Jamaica
Villain causes harm	A	Agents killed, dumped in sea
Mediation	B	Misfortune known, hero dispatched
Hero gets magic agent	F	Bond gets new gun
Hero leaves home	↑	Bond flies to Jamaica
Hero is attacked	H	Poison fruit, centipede, etc.
Hero led to object of search	G	Bond and Quarrel go to Island
Hero is pursued	Pr	No's men search for Bond on island
Difficult task proposed	M	Escape by traversing shaft
The villain is punished	U	Bond kills Dr. No
Hero(ine) new appearance	T	Honeychile's nose is fixed
Hero is married	W	Bond and Honeychile make love

makes his way down the shaft, outwitting the various devices Dr. No has installed in the shaft designed to kill anyone trying to escape, and lands in the sea. He overpowers some guards in a huge cavern where Dr. No is overseeing the loading of guano, buries Dr. No under a huge pile of guano and escapes with Honeychile to the mainland, where he has her nose fixed by a surgeon and then makes love to her.

We find in this story a number of Proppian functions. I will not offer as complete an analysis as I could make (in that this could involve numerous functions) but indicate some of the most important ones.

This Proppian analysis could have been extended considerably and made more detailed by dealing with other events in the novel and subcategories that Propp discusses in his book. But I believe I have made my point already. Propp's functions can be applied to contemporary narrative fictions successfully, often with relatively little adaptation. *Dr. No* and other spy stories and stories from other genres are, in reality, modernized and transformed fairy tales and perform many of the same functions for contemporary young people and adults that fairy tales do for children.

Dr. No and the Negation
of the Negation

I have, to this point, offered a synopsis of the plot of *Dr. No* and shown how it is composed of elements similar to those found in fairy tales. It is, we see, possible to use Propp's functions to analyze the book syntagmatically. Now I would like to offer a paradigmatic analysis of the text, an analysis which elicits patterns of oppositions found in the story that give it meaning. I do not believe that Fleming, when he wrote *Dr. No*, was aware of this pattern nor do I believe that readers of the story bring this pattern of oppositions to consciousness. But I do think readers undergo a process of making, below the level of awareness, bipolar oppositions that are applied to all characters and actions in the story.

There is, let me suggest, a structure, a set of relationships in *Dr. No* that gives it meaning. Remember, our concern here is not with what characters do or say, but what they mean. The title of the book, *Dr. No*, and its leading villain are most useful here. Dr. No, as his name suggests, stands for negation. He explains his name as follows: "I changed my name to Julius No—the Julius after my father and the No for my rejection of all authority" (Fleming, 1958, p. 138). He had earlier described how he "loved death and the destruction of people and things" (p. 139). One other comment he makes is particularly interesting here. "I was entertained," he says "by the idea of converting bird dung into gold" (p. 139).

The basic polarity in this book, I would suggest, involves negation, on one side, and the positiveness of our heroine, Honeychile Rider, on the other. We must remember, also, that as Lévi-Strauss (1967) has suggested, one of the basic functions of mythic heroes is to resolve contradictions, to mediate between opposing forces. The polarity in this book, then, is not between Bond and Dr. No but between Honeychile Rider and Dr. No.

Table 2.5 shows the ideational armature upon which the narrative is strung and suggests how Bond, as his name suggests, is a mediating figure between these two polarities. When Bond seizes

TABLE 2.5 Bipolar Oppositions in *Dr. No*

Honey	Feces
Honeychile Rider	Dr. No (Dr. GuaNO)
Positiveness of nature	Negativeness of nature
Nature girl	Machine-man combination
Purity	Half-Breed (Dr. No, Chigroes)
Innocence (chile)	Knowledge (Dr.)
Goddess	Fiend
Initiated	Initiator
Love	Torture
Child figure	Father figure
Perfected	Eliminated

control of the giant crane that is loading guano onto a ship and releases the guano onto Dr. No, we have a negation of a negation that becomes an affirmation. The relationship between gold and feces is, I might add, one that Freud has discussed in an essay he wrote on anal eroticism. In archaic stories and myths, he tells us, gold, the most valuable thing we have, and feces, the least valuable one, are related.

I have not dealt with the racism, sexism, or other sociological and cultural aspects of this text. Fleming's description of Chigroes, who Dr. No more or less breeds for his own purposes, as having "some of the intelligence of the Chinese and most of the vices of the black man" is overtly racist (Fleming, 1958, p. 52). His creation of Honeychile, a childlike goddess with a broken nose (from being raped), is a sexist fantasy that appeals to the fantasies of many men (the goddess who cannot judge their sexual performance). And Dr. No's personality and life history, as delineated by his creator, Ian Fleming, is a gold mine for the psychiatrist and psychopathologist. Those interested in the social and psychological aspect of James Bond are advised to consult Tony Bennett and Janet Woollacott's (1987) excellent study, *Bond and Beyond: The Political Career of a Popular Hero.*

NBC's "Cosby Show" and Fox's "In Living Color" are very different half-hour comedy shows controlled primarily by black performers. Bill Cosby's humor tends to be warm and gently didactic: eat your veggies; stay in school. Keenen Ivory Wayan's approach is hip-hop brash and iconoclastic; neither whites nor blacks are exempt. But both shows share a distinctively black sensibility, and that's because the stars also serve as executive producers, making sure that they will not be trapped in the business-as-usual land of sitcom.

Consider the more typical sitcoms. Too often lacking any kind of sensibility, black or white, they are instead constructed on what television executives call a high concept, which usually means a totally unbelievable situation steeped in gross exaggeration. Glue it all together, guys, the executives might say, and lets see if it can crawl up the ratings charts.

SOURCE: O'Connor, J. J. (1990, October 4). Black Sitcoms Steeped in Concept. *New York Times*. Copyright © 1990 by The New York Times Company. Reprinted by permission.

3

Formulas and Texts

This chapter defines formulas and deals with their use in mass-mediated texts. It considers the relationship that exists between genres, which are understood as "kinds of texts" and formulas, which are understood as "conventions" used in structuring texts. It also deals with the ideas of a number of theorists who have written on genres and formulas.

On the Nature of Formulas

In the *Six-Gun Mystique*, an early study of the nature of formulaic literature, John G. Cawelti (a humanities professor from the University of Chicago) suggests that there are three approaches or "major forms of deterministic interpretation" that critics have used in recent years. The first approach deals with literature as a "reflection of the dominant intellectual and political concerns of a period, and of the special and unique characteristics of a race or culture" (1971, p. 4).

The second approach is Marxist or Freudian criticism which argues that "literature can best be understood and analyzed through the way in which it accomplishes certain social or psychological functions" (1971, p. 7). These functions involve the way works reflect political ideologies or various unconscious drives and related phenomena.

The third approach is the formulaic one. Cawelti offers a number of different definitions and explanations of what he means by formulaic. He reveals himself a universalist in that he argues what is important is not the individual text but the formula: "the culturally significant phenomenon is not the individual work, but the formula or recipe by which more or less anonymous producers turn out individual novels or films" (p. 25). His initial definition of the formula is "a conventional system for structuring cultural products. It can be distinguished from invented structures which are new ways of organizing works of art" (p. 29). Cawelti argues that works of art contain two elements—conventions and inventions—and that formulaic works are essentially conventional, guided by rules and codes which both those who create works of art and those who consume them know.

Cawelti makes a distinction between genres, which he interprets in a more or less traditional way (basing his ideas on the work of the Canadian literary theorist Northrop Frye), and formulas. Frye (1957) believes that myths are universal patterns of action that are found in all cultures. Cawelti (1971) writes that

> genre can be defined as a structural pattern which embodies a universal pattern or myth in the materials of language. Formula, on the other hand, is cultural; it represents the way in which a particular culture has embodied both mythical archetypes and its own preoccupations in a narrative form. (p. 30)

Formulas, from Cawelti's perspective, are tied to specific countries and periods of time and have a much more narrowly defined "repertory of plots, characters and setting" (p. 31).

Formulas are important, Cawelti adds, because formulaic stories enable individuals in a given society to deal with various unconscious imperatives, repressed desires and other material of a similar nature. He then adds to his previous definition of formulas:

My argument, then, is that formula stories like the detective story, the Western, the seduction novel, the biblical epic, and many others are structures of narrative conventions which carry out a variety of cultural functions in a unified way. We can best define these formulas as principles for the selection of certain plots, characters, and settings, which possess in addition to their basic narrative structure the dimensions of collective ritual, game and dream. (p. 33)

There are some problems with Cawelti's notion of genres involving mythical archetypes. In part because he does not fully explain where these archetypes come from. Cawelti mentions the ideas of a critic, Sheldon Sacks, who argues that genres are known intuitively by everyone in that, he claims, we all have an innate capacity to differentiate between the comic and the tragic.

I would suggest we use the term *genre* to cover the various kinds of texts that Cawelti sees as formulaic—westerns, spy stories, detective stories, and so forth and understand formulas to involve the various conventions found in various genres and subgenres. The formula is considerably different in hard-boiled detective stories and in classical, deductive genius (Sherlock Holmes, Hercules Poirot) detective stories.

Formulas involve the following aspects of texts:

Time. They generally take place at a certain time. For example, a western has to take place at the turn of the century.

Location. They take place in a specific place. Westerns take place on the edge of the frontier.

Heroes. They have certain kinds of heroes. Westerns have cowboys, who may be innocent and never shoot first.

Heroines. The heroines have specific qualities and attributes. In westerns we have schoolmarms, bar hostesses, and so forth.

Villains. The villains have distinctive characteristics. Different kinds of westerns have different villains: the corrupt sheriff, the psychotic killer, the savage Indian, the criminal banker.

Secondary Characters. They tend to have certain needs, and so forth. In westerns, they are the townsfolk, who are too weak to resist criminal or savage elements that are attacking or controlling them.

Plots. Plots vary from genre to genre. In the western, the plot usually involves actions that restore law and order—gunfights, chases, and so forth.

Themes. Different genres focus on different themes. In the typical western, it involves justice.

Costume. Different genres involve different dress. In the western, we have cowboy hats, boots, and so forth.

Locomotion. There are different means of locomotion in different genres. In the western, it is the horse that is dominant.

Weaponry. There are different kinds of weapons for each genre. In the western it is the six-gun.

The different genres traditionally have different kinds of heroes, plots, themes, costumes, and so forth, depending upon the conventions that have been established over the years and the logic of circumstances. Thus, for example, the hard-boiled detective story tends to be urban, has a tough-guy detective, who gets into fights, carries a pistol (perhaps a .45, never a six-gun) and traditionally rescues damsels in distress and, at the same time, solves a murder or series of murders. Spy stories, on the other hand, have an international flavor and take place in various cities all over the world, involve men who work for large organizations, use pistols with silencers, and involve stealing secrets, finding moles, and so forth. Table 3.1 suggests some of the dominant traits of some important popular genres.

The phenomena discussed above may, for the most part, be seen as semiotic signifiers of specific genres. Saussure (1966) divided the sign into two components: a *signifier* (sound or image) and a

TABLE 3.1 Formulaic Elements in Popular Genres

Genre	Western	Science Fiction	Hard-Boiled Detective	Spy
Time	1800s	Future	Present	Present
Location	Edge of civilization	Space	City	World
Hero	Cowboy	Spaceman	Detective	Agent
Heroine	Schoolmarm	Spacegal	Damsel in distress	Woman spy
Secondary characters	Townsfolk, indians	Technicians	Cops, criminals	Other spies
Villains	Outlaws	Aliens	Killers	Moles
Plot	Restore law	Repel aliens	Find killer	Find mole
Theme	Justice progress	Triumph of humanity	Discovery of killer	Save free world
Costume	Cowboy hat	High-tech	Raincoat	Suit
Locomotion	Horse	Spaceship	Beat up car	Planes
Weaponry	Six-gun	Ray gun	Pistol, fists	Pistol & silencer

signified (concept). The relation that exists between a signified and signifier, he added, is arbitrary, based on convention, and not something that is natural or universal. Many of the phenomena in the table are visual, which means it is possible for writers and producers of films and television shows to establish, very quickly and economically, the genres they are using. Once we see a rocket ship (a signifier) hurtling through space, for example, we know that we are dealing with science fiction (a signified).

A cowboy hat is not, by itself, enough to establish the certainty that a story one is watching is a western. But a man in a cowboy hat in a small town, on the edge of civilization in a society in which there are horses and stagecoaches, Indians, and so forth does signify a western. Some of the characters in *Dallas*, a soap opera, wore cowboy hats . . . but that does not mean that *Dallas* was a western. It was, instead, a modern soap opera that took place in a western city.

Reader and Viewer Expectations

A table like Table 3.1 could be made for all the other popular genres as well. What it shows, in a highly abbreviated way, are the various conventions found in the four genres—conventions that readers of novels or viewers of films or television shows learn and expect to find in each genre text they read or see. Of course there are all kinds of variations and modifications that are possible within a given genre, but as Cawelti (1971) points out, if a writer inserts too many inventions in a given text, readers will find their expectations not fulfilled and may become confused.

Cawelti mentions the matter of repetition compulsion, the need that certain neurotics have to repeat certain actions over and over again as a means of dealing with their anxieties. People who like detective stories and other works in the various popular genres may have elements of this repetition compulsion in their personalities or, may gain certain satisfactions from particular genres and subgenres. Thus, when they choose to view a spy story, detective story, romance, or any other genre, they do not want to find too many deviations from the classic formulations to which they have become accustomed. Readers bring expectations and knowledge to their reading (and viewers to their viewing) that must be taken into account. Recent work by "reader response" theorists has suggested that the focus on the intentions and creative powers of writers (and in the visual media, directors, and producers) neglects the role readers play in making sense of (or decoding, to use the jargon) texts.

As the result of constant reading and viewing of texts in various genres, readers and viewers discern patterns and formulas that define the genres and differentiate them from other genres. These conventions are well-known and in some cases, such as detective stories and romance novels, have been listed and discussed in articles and books.

In the case of a classic radio western, the *Lone Ranger*, George Steiner (an original cast member of the radio show), describes the formula used by Fran Striker, who wrote the scripts. In 1939, incidentally, Striker was writing an estimated 60,000 words a week. He was assisted by a small staff in writing 156 *Lone Ranger* scripts a year as well as 356 newspaper cartoons.

Here is Striker's formula for the *Lone Ranger*.

1. Establish a character.
2. Give him a problem he can't solve.
3. Explain why he can't solve it and that involves the villain.
4. The Lone Ranger learns about the situation.
5. The antagonist learns that the Ranger is going to interfere.
6. The antagonist plots to kill the Ranger.
7. The Ranger outwits or outfights the crooks and survives.
8. The Ranger solves the situation. (Steiner, 1991, p. 116)

As Steiner points out, Striker did not do every show in that order. The elements can be shifted around, though Steiner estimates that one out of every five shows did conform to this pattern.

Under each element, there are varying possibilities (just as Propp showed a number of different variations for each function). Thus the character can be an old man, a young man, an old woman, a young woman. As Steiner writes, "when you take them in all of their possible combinations you have 8 to the 10th power of possible plots. The thing could go on forever" (p. 116).

It is this formulaic plot structure that enables those who write for the mass media to grind out stories so quickly. What modern genre writers do, in effect, is think of variations on the basic plot: in one episode, the person needing help is an old lady, in the next a young child, and so on ad infinitum.

Is There an Ideal-Type Genre?

I would like to recall the previous discussion of realism and nominalism. Are only particular things "real" (whatever that may mean) or are "types" or "classes" of things, such as genres, also real? In a similar light might we ask whether all the genres and subgenres are created out of some prototypic genre, some ideal genre that contains the basic form out of which all the other genres are spun.

This is highly speculative, of course, but as we evolve from infants to adults, we come into contact with printed narratives in the following order (very approximately): board books (toddlers), picture books (preschoolers), fairy tales, generally illustrated (ages 5 to 7), beginning readers (1st and 2nd grade), chapter books (books with chapters, 2nd grade and on), books in series—children get security from having a familiar author (2nd and 3rd grades), and all kinds of different books thereafter.

When it comes to narratives, in general, let me suggest the following order:

1. Dreams
Books
2. Lullabies and songs
3. Board books, picture books, story books
4. Fairy tales
5. Novels
Mass Media
6. Television serials, video games, etc.
7. Plays
8. Radio shows
9. Television shows
10. Films

The order of the last four or five items may vary and some people may have very little experience with plays (defined here as live theatre). What is different about the last four items from all the

TABLE 3.2 Elements in Genres From Fairy Tales

Genre	*Elements From Fairy Tales*
Science fiction	Magical agents, magical powers, etc.; hero leaves home
Detective	Finding kidnapped heroines
Soap operas	Relations between members of families
Spy stories	Finding false heroes; Hero (unrecognized) arrives in a foreign country
Situation comedies	Reversal of problem stories about royal families; stories about tricksters
Western	Hero and villain fight, a chase (reversed, with villain pursued)

others is that they are all based on scripts and involve dialogue, sound effects, and so forth.

I would like to suggest, as a hypothesis, that our first narratives are found in our dreams. And we all dream, constantly—even though we often do not remember the dreams when we wake. In these dreams we are the heroes and heroines (or the victims or both) and it is our adventures in these dreams that establish the pattern upon which other narratives and various genres are set.

It may be because fairy tales are so intimately connected to our psychic processes and dreams and so universal that explains why they are so important to people. They may be the first significant narratives we encounter; Bruno Bettelheim (1975), a distinguished psychologist who wrote *The Uses of Enchantment: The Meaning and Importance of Fairy Tales*, suggests this is the case. He is rather negative about story books that are read to very young children and that, he suggests, do not give them the kinds of messages and gratifications that they need. It is the fairy tale that speaks to the needs of young children and it is here that I think we find manifested the prototypic tale from which other tales and genres evolve.

TABLE 3.3 Dreams as Prototypes for Narratives

Id	Superego
The hero	The villain
Young	Old
Quests	Deters
Desire	Guilt (in pathological form)
Fights villains	Fights heroes
Magic aspects	Antimagic
Displacement	
Condensation	
Marries princess	Tries to prevent marriage

Let us consider some of the more important mass-mediated fictional genres and the elements of those genres in which fairy tales may provide some contribution. The suggestion is, then, that many of the elements found in the most important genres are found in fairy tales and different genres focus upon different aspects of fairy tales.

Relation of Intra-Psychic Elements to Narratives

Let me propose an additional hypothesis, namely that narratives stem from conflicts in the psyche, in dreams we all have, between what Freud described as the Id (our drives) and what he described as the Superego (our consciences and the upholder of traditional morality).

This hypothesis would generate the structure illustrated in Table 3.3.

In his book, *An Elementary Textbook of Psychoanalysis*, Charles Brenner (1974) supports this contention. He discusses

> the powerful and long lasting effect that childhood instinctual wishes have on mental life.... In many instances it is more precise to say that these effects do not result directly from the instinctual wishes and

conflicts themselves, but rather from the fantasies which arise from them. . . . Among the consequences of childhood instinctual fantasies are daydreams and stories of all kinds: fairy tales, myths, legends, and literary productions at every level of sophistication and excellence. Fairy tales and similar stories are usually the first that interest a child. (p. 203)

These stories, Brenner points out, deal primarily with Oedipal themes. A young and weak hero (or heroine) triumphs over and often kills a wicked old villain, marries a beautiful princess (or handsome prince) and lives happily ever after. There are numerous variations on this theme but generally speaking a smaller, weaker, younger figure defeats a seemingly more powerful, older villainous one.

Brenner discusses a number of different fairy tales in his book and relates them to Oedipal themes. He suggests, in fact, that all narratives are ultimately connected to Oedipal themes. He writes that

for a literary work to have a strong, or, even more, a lasting appeal, its plot must arouse and gratify some important aspect of the unconscious oedipal wishes of the members of its audience. (p. 235)

If the child is father to the man or mother to the woman, the child (or, more precisely, childhood instinctual wishes and desire) is also father or mother to the writer of narratives, whatever the level of sophistication and genre. This Oedipal relationship of the characters in stories is generally highly disguised, cleverly camouflaged, and not recognized by the members of the audience (nor created consciously by the writer) but it is there, felt by all involved with the texts, and recognizable to those who understand the way the psyche works.

We do not have a hero with a thousand faces so much as a hero with a thousand parts in a thousand dramas (actually, thousands of dramas if you count our dreams) and that hero or heroine is each of us and all the stories we read and see are, ultimately, our stories.

Why Fairy Tales Mean So Much

Bruno Bettelheim (1975) discusses the classical formula in fairy tales, writing that

> the fairy tale begins with the hero at the mercy of those who think little of him and his abilities, who mistreat him and even threaten his life, as the wicked queen does in "Snow White." As the story unfolds, the hero is often forced to depend on friendly helpers: creatures of the underworld like the dwarfs in "Snow White," or magic animals like the birds in "Cinderella." At the tale's end the hero has mastered all trials and despite them remained true to himself, or in successfully undergoing them has achieved his true selfhood. He has become an autocrat in the best sense of the word—a self-ruler, a truly autonomous person, not a person who rules over others. (p. 127)

The hero becomes an autonomous person, marries the princess and we know little else other than that everyone "lived happily ever after." These stories are immensely satisfying to young children because they show children that they can triumph over difficulties that disturb them, find someone to love, establish a home for themselves, and have a secure and happy life.

Curiously enough, there seems to be no other genre that helps us deal with the various psychological pressures and anxieties that plague us all as successfully as fairy tales. The only literary works that give us the same kind of relief and satisfaction are the great novels and works of theatre, many of which, not surprisingly, also deal with Oedipal themes.

Thanks to the Greeks, we can distinguish tragedy from comedy in drama, and so we still tend to assume that each is the half of drama that is not the other half. When we come to deal with such forms as the masque, opera, movie, ballet, puppet-play, mystery-play, morality, commedia dell'arte, and lauber-spiel, we find ourselves in the position of the Renaissance doctors who refused to treat syphilis because Galen said nothing about it.

SOURCE: Frye, N. (1957). *Anatomy of Criticism*. Princeton, NJ: Princeton University Press.

4

Genre Theory

On Formulas and Genres

As I use the terms, a *genre* is more comprehensive than a *formula*. Consider the mystery, for example. Within this genre, one might have a number of different kinds of mysteries—tough guy detectives, Sherlock Holmesian types with powerful minds and remarkable powers of deduction, police procedurals, and so on. Each of these would be a subgenre with a somewhat different formula, though each would involve solving some mystery and discovering, generally speaking, who the murderer is (or, in some cases, who the murderers are).

It is possible to have detectives solve other kinds of mysteries—find missing letters or other documents, discover who stole something valuable, for example—but most frequently there is some kind of a murder involved in mysteries. Why might this be? If you accept the thesis that Oedipal drives are behind our interest in various genres, the need for a murder is obvious. Also, many murder mysteries involve finding a murderer before he or she strikes again, which generates much more tension and excitement in readers and audiences than other kinds of detecting tasks.

Douglas Kellner (1980) offers a slightly different definition of the term *genre*. He writes, in "Television Images, Codes and Messages" that

> a genre consists of a coded set of formulas and conventions which indicate a culturally accepted way of organizing material into distinct patterns. Once established, genres dictate the basic conditions of cultural production and reception. For example, crime dramas invariably have a violent crime, a search for its perpetrators, and often a chase, fight, or bloody elimination of the criminal, communicating the message "crime does not pay." The audience comes to expect these predictable pleasures and a crime drama "code" develops, enshrined in production studio texts and practices. (vol. 7, no. 4)

Audiences develop certain expectations for genres based on viewing texts and figuring out (decoding) their conventions. When people talk about television shows, they generally talk about a particular episode of a specific show and its genre. Knowing the genre enables us to anticipate what a particular show in that genre will be like. This is quite important for most television viewers and filmgoers.

One problem involved with classifying works into genres is that different people establish different typologies. For example, in *Genreflecting: a Guide to Reading Interests in Genre Fiction*, Betty Rosenberg (1986) subsumes mysteries (tough guy as well as cerebral or "classical") under a more general heading, "Thrillers." Rosenberg is a librarian who is interested in genre literature, a kind of literature that, as she points out, most librarians consider to be trash. Her list of kinds of detective stories follows in a slightly abbreviated manner:

THRILLER
    Themes and types
      Detective story and detective
      Police detective
      Private detective
      Amateur detectives (doctor, lawyer, rogue or thief, ecclesiastical, English aristocrat, academic)

Woman detective
Immortal investigators
Mystery-suspense, Psychological-suspense
Crime/Caper
Spy/Espionage
Financial intrigue/Espionage
Political intrigue/Espionage (1986, p. 3)

Her book is interesting and useful, but I would argue that her classification system is inadequate, in that it takes a characteristic of a number of fictional genres—creating thrills and suspense—and elevates this aspect of these genres to the status of a genre itself. Classifications have to have two qualities if they are to be useful: they must be exhaustive (covering everything) and all categories have to be mutually exclusive.

As we have seen, the formulas for detective stories and spy stories in their most classical formulations are quite different. It is possible, of course, for a detective like Hercules Poirot to be involved in a mystery involving spies and for spies to have to solve some kind of a mystery (who's the mole?) but the two kinds of stories are quite different and are not subcategories of thrillers, at least as I see things. It also does not make sense to have "Themes and Types" as one category.

Classifying things is a way of making sense out of chaos (or seeming chaos). But every system of classification has a bias in it—the system of classification affects what we see and do not see and shapes the way we see things.

Genres and Order

In *American Television Genres*, Stuart M. Kaminsky and Jeffrey H. Mahan (1986) suggest that one reason we are interested in genres is because human beings seem to have a need to classify things. "The word *genre* simply means order," they write. "All things are ordered by human beings so that they can be dealt with" (p. 17). I will not deal with the question of whether the order we find in

things is in the things themselves and thus is discovered or whether
the order is in our minds and is arbitrarily imposed on things by
us. Whatever the case, we seem to have a "rage" for order in that
by ordering things we help make sense of things and can function
more intelligently.

We may find that different people or groups of people order their
universes differently and that there is consensus only in some
areas. Whatever the case, we all seem to have a need to classify
objects and put them into groupings of one sort or another. This
need may be connected to the point Saussure made; namely that
concepts acquire meaning in terms of their relations with other
terms in some system and the most important relationship involves
being what others are not.

As Kaminsky and Mahan (1986) write:

> When we encounter any work of popular art, whether it is a nursery
> rhyme from near antiquity or television coverage of a baseball game,
> we are dealing with an apparent contradiction. The work of popular
> art is two things at the same time: it is like many other things that
> have preceded it; yet, is also unique, not a precise duplication of
> anything that has been presented before. This leads to the basic debate
> about whether examination of works of popular art, or any art, should
> emphasize their familiarity or their uniqueness. (p. 3)

We need a certain amount of stability in our lives, which means
that repetition is valuable to us, but we also long for variation and
innovation, which is why we like serial works—the repetition of
the form provides security but the variation in plot provides emotional excitement for us.

Let me suggest that works of narrative art (and other kinds of art
as well) form a continuum. At one end of the continuum we have
absolute originality and uniqueness (to the extent that this is possible). At the other end of the continuum we find slavish repetition
of well-known formulas. People find things difficult at either extreme. If they encounter something totally unlike anything they
have ever encountered before, they are confused and mystified.
(And have to resort to books that explain *Ulysses* or, as an even

better example, *Finnegan's Wake*.) If they encounter something totally familiar, they can be bored very easily.

Intertextuality

Thus, most works (and Cawelti [1971] pointed this out) fall somewhere between the extremes of convention and invention. Genre works tend to be conventional; works of elite art often are closer to the inventive pole. There is a question, however, about how far we can go in inventing narratives that are really new. Can we actually create a text that is really new and different? If we can do so, will we still be able to communicate to others?

Some critics use the term *intertextuality* to suggest that all texts are related to all other texts, even though they may not consciously borrow from a given text or formula or genre (though in some cases texts do quote from other texts).

Parody, of course, is a prime example of intertextuality; in parody we imitate and poke fun at styles of authors or filmmakers, specific texts, or kinds of texts, that is—genres. It is, of course, possible to ridicule styles, texts, and genres all at the same time. The list below offers examples of parodies for each of the classifications.

Parody of style:	Hemingway parodies.	Spoof of Hemingway's writing style.
Parody of text:	*Hardware Wars*.	Spoof of *Star Wars*.
Parody of genre:	*Twin Peaks*.	Spoof of soap operas.

In order to be able to make a parody of an author or text or genre, there must be something distinctive and recognizable about them, which the humorist can take off on. Parody depends, to a considerable degree, upon readers and audiences recognizing what is being imitated and ridiculed, though people can still (to a limited extent) enjoy parodies without being familiar with a given style or text. Generally speaking people can recognize when a genre is being parodied because we are so familiar with the genres carried by the mass media.

Parody also involves more than just imitation; there must be other techniques of humor employed, such as exaggeration, mimicry, absurdity, and word play. Every year, for example, there are contests for the best Hemingway parodies and quotations from the winning selections, which ridicule Hemingway's distinctive style of writing, are generally run in newspapers.

Umberto Eco on Seriality

Umberto Eco (1985), the distinguished Italian semiotician and novelist, has written an essay, "Innovation and Repetition: Between Modern and Post-Modern Aesthetics," which is of interest to us here. This essay, which appeared in the Fall 1985 issue on "The Moving Image" in *Daedalus* magazine, deals with the matter of *seriality* and its relation to modern aesthetic theory. He points out that in classical periods, novelty was not given a high status and the differences between so-called major and minor arts were not stressed. He writes that

> classical aesthetics was not so anxious for innovation at any cost: on the contrary, it frequently appreciated as "beautiful" the good tokens of an everlasting type. . . . This is the reason why modern aesthetics was so severe apropos the industrial-like products of the mass media. A popular song, a TV commercial, a comic strip, a detective novel, a Western movie were seen as more or less successful tokens of a given model or type. As such they were judged pleasurable but non-artistic. . . . The products of the mass media were equated with the products of industry insofar as they were produced *in series*, the "serial" production was considered as alien to the artistic invention. (p. 162)

The works created for the mass media were based on such things as redundancy (which was seen as the opposite of information), repetition, iteration, and following an established schema. But as Eco points out, even the 19th-century writers tended to be repetitive, with a fundamental pattern that did not vary very much.

What we call a postmodern aesthetics, Eco suggests, represents an attempt to deal with the matter of iteration and repetition and the "new aesthetics of seriality." He offers a typology of different kinds of repetition in the arts, showing that there are differences among them (unlike books in which one copy is an exact replica of another).

The Retake. Here we use the characters from a previous adventure but show what happens to them after the first adventure has ended. He offers examples such as *Star Wars* and *Superman* in which familiar characters are engaged in new adventures.

The Remake. This represents retelling of a given story. He points out that Shakespeare remade preceding stories, demonstrating that one can remake without repeating. In recent years there have been a number of remakes of *King Kong* and other films as well.

The Series. A series involves familiar "fixed" or "pivotal" characters around whom different secondary characters turn, generating the sense that new stories are being created while, in truth, Eco says, the "narrative scheme does not change" (1985, p. 268). We enjoy the novelty of the differences in the stories and gain the pleasure of familiarity with a narrative that really is not different. As examples of series he offers *All in the Family, Colombo.* One could add television series, Sherlock Holmes stories, books about the heroics of Hercules Poirot, and so on. There are variations on the series format: flashbacks, which deal with a character's life at some earlier period of his or her development; loop-series, which involve characters in continually reliving their past; spirals, in which characters continually repeat their standard performances (thereby enriching and deepening our understanding with them); and finally powerful dramatic personalities like John Wayne, who seem to always make the same film over and over again.

The Saga. Eco suggests sagas involve the activities of a family over time. In sagas, people age and evolve. Sagas are, of course,

serial in nature, but they are more or less disguised forms of serials.
He cites *Dallas* as a typical example of the saga.

Eco then discusses "Intertextual Dialogue," which he describes
as "the phenomenon by which a given text echoes previous texts"
(1985, p. 170). He is specifically interested, here, in echoes that are
explicit and recognizable—that is, quotations (so to speak) which
use intertextuality to gain certain effects and which assume that
readers of books or viewers of films or television programs will
recognize the quotations. This technique used to be found mostly
in experimental art but it now is found in the mass media. We find
this, for example, in commercials that refer to other texts (such as
the famous Macintosh "1984" commercial, which was related to
Orwell's novel, *1984*, and other commercials and texts, as well).
These considerations lead Eco to suggest a modern aesthetic
solution to the problem of seriality and repetition in the arts.

> Let us now try to review the phenomena listed above from the point
> of view of a "modern" conception of aesthetic value, according to
> which every work aesthetically "well done" is endowed with two
> characteristics:
>
> 1. It must achieve a dialectic between order and novelty—in
>   other words between scheme and innovation;
> 2. This dialectic must be perceived by the consumer, who must
>   not only grasp the contents of the message, but also the way
>   in which the message transmits these contents.
>
> This being the case, nothing prevents the types of repetition listed
> above from achieving the conditions necessary to the realization of
> aesthetic value, and the history of the arts is ready to furnish us with
> satisfactory examples for each of the types in our classification. (pp.
> 173, 174)

Eco then takes his schema and shows how it applies to many works
of classic literature such as Ariosto's *Orlando Furioso*, the works of
Shakespeare, and Balzac's *Human Comedy*. He shows that many
works in literature, the arts, the mass media are continually quoting
from other works that preceded them. The arts are full of parodies,
plagiarisms, retakes, remakes, and ironic intertextual jokes.

When he comes to television serials, Eco raises another issue. He moves on from his discussion of the problems of order and innovation in the media. Serial texts mirror the routines of everyday life and are "infinite," he suggests, in that they are capable of endless change and variation. Postmodern aesthetics, he argues, recognizes this infinite variability but instead of celebrating novelty and innovation, moves in a different direction and celebrates the stylistic techniques by which the periodical, the regular and the continuous are shown.

He discusses the work of an Italian thinker, Omar Calabrese, who argues that we are witnessing a new aesthetic sensibility, a neobaroque or post-postmodern one, based on "the articulation of the elementary narrative structures [that] can migrate in combinations of the highest improbability around the various characters." The focus seems to be not on the possibilities of scheme and variation (which was the defense of the apologists for the mass media) but on scheme-variation, in which "the variation is no longer more appreciable than the scheme" (p. 180). What this seems to mean is that we have returned to an aesthetic based on similarity and unity, not difference and diversity.

Yuri Lotman on the Aesthetics of Identity and Aesthetics of Opposition

Yuri Lotman (1977), the distinguished Russian semiotician and literary theorist, offers a slightly different approach to thinking about genres. He makes a distinction between the "aesthetics of identity" and the "aesthetics of opposition." In *The Structure of The Artistic Text* he suggests that all kinds of works of art and literary works can be divided into two classes.

> The first class consists of artistic phenomena whose structures are given beforehand; the audience's expectations are met by the entire construction of the work.
> Throughout the history of art, artistic systems that associate aesthetic worth with originality are the exception rather than the rule.

> The folklore of all nations, medieval art . . . *commedia dell'arte,*
> Classicism—there are only a few of the artistic systems which judge
> a work according to its observation of certain rules rather [than] their
> violation. The rules governing word choice and the construction of
> the metaphors, rituals of narration, strictly defined possibilities for
> plot combinations that are known in advance, and *loci communi*
> (whole pieces of frozen text) all form a very special artistic system.
> (p. 289)

What is important, Lotman adds, is that audience not only know a
set of possibilities but that they also know a set of impossibilities
"standing in paired opposition to the first set on each level of the
artistic construction" (p. 289).

These works, that are tied to the identification of depicted phenomena with model-clichés that audiences know beforehand, are
based, Lotman says, on the aesthetics of identity. The other class
of texts is what Lotman (1977) describes as reflecting the aesthetics
of opposition.

> The other class of structures we find on this level are systems whose
> code is unknown to the audience before the act of artistic perception
> begins. This is the aesthetic of opposition rather than identity. The
> author sets his own, original resolution, which he believes to be the
> truer one, in opposition to methods of modelling reality that are
> familiar to the reader. (p. 292)

At first sight this might seem to be an attempt by the author
to reject cultural norms, to create "without rules." But, argues
Lotman, this is impossible. He writes that

> creation independent of rules and structural relations is impossible.
> This would contradict the nature of a work of art as a model and a
> sign; it would make it impossible to understand the world with the
> help of art and to convey the results of that understanding to an
> audience. (p. 292)

One can fight against a particular system, but not against the
principle of system*ness*. What we find in works based on the
aesthetics of opposition is not, to adopt a game metaphor, a game

without rules but a game, as Lotman puts it, "whose rules must be established in the process of play" (p. 292).

Understanding these two aesthetics, or, in our terms, the significance of genre, enables us to evaluate texts better Lotman suggests. We expect certain rules or codes to be employed in some genres (folk epics, fairy tales) where they are appropriate; if we find them in other genres, such as a social novel, we can question whether they belong there. Also, readers prepare themselves for certain kinds of texts on the basis of signifiers like titles, authors, and genres; they have certain expectations about what these texts will be like. In these works, the "structure" tends to be manifest in the text, not outside of it, which is often the case with works from the aesthetics of opposition. What we have called narrative genres tend to fall within the aesthetics of identity and are found in what is called *popular culture*.

There are several significant points in Lotman's theory. First, he points out that one can never have a text that breaks all the rules that people can understand. You can avoid a given system (or set of conventions in a text) but you must have *some* system. Also, we have had formulaic texts, repetitive texts, for a long time; they are not something new, spawned by the electronic mass media. Finally, Lotman stresses the importance of the "reader" (by which we mean person who reads a book, watches a television program or film) in the scheme of things. Authors generally have their readers in mind when they write and it is the kind of reader one hopes to appeal to that plays an important part in the way a text is created.

Strategies of Generic Criticism
of Narratives

We are now at a point in which we can consider a number of different approaches that the critic of narrative texts and genres can adapt. There is no one way of analyzing texts and genres, no royal road to criticism. A great deal depends upon the text itself and the interests of the critic. Some texts lend themselves to one or another aspect of analysis while other texts require a number of different approaches. We can, for example, focus on the way the texts reflect social and political matters, on the text's formulaic elements, on the intertextual aspects of the text, on the nature of its seriality, on its style and the aesthetic codes that are found in it.

A more comprehensive list of approaches a critic may take follows.

1. A historical study of the evolution of a genre. When, for example, did soap operas start and how have they evolved and changed over the years? This approach also generally involves a good deal of description, so readers get some kind of an idea of what early texts were like.

2. Relation of a text to a genre. How does a given text (which may be a series, such as *Dallas*) relate to the soap opera genre. In analyzing a series we have to figure out how to select a representative sampling of it or characterize it. That is, in a series we have to decide what the text is—the series or, perhaps, a significant episode from the series. We also have to consider whether it offers any innovations that are significant in any way.

3. A study of how genres relate to one another. Are there cases in which conventions and styles associated with one genre (mysteries) have impacted on other genres (soaps)? If so, what does this tell us about the media, the problems of creative artists, and the cultures and societies in which these genres are found.

4. Relation of television shows or films of a given period to one another, as far as styles and themes and other matters found in the genres are concerned.

5. Comparison of American texts and genres with texts and genres from other countries? There are considerable differences, for example, between American and English mysteries. What are the differences and what do they reflect about values, attitudes, belief systems, and so forth in American and English culture and society?

6. Distinctive aspects of heroes and heroines (and villains and villainesses) in the various genres? How do they differ? In what ways, if any, are they similar? What social and psychological functions might these characters have?

7. Analysis of what different genres reflect about society and culture? Do certain genres, for example, appeal to certain socioeconomic classes, to certain racial and ethnic groups, to certain genders, regions, age groups, subcultures, and so forth.

8. Impact of mythic and folkloristic content on texts and genres. Are certain genres more likely to use myths and folklore than others? If so, why? What is the relationship between myth, folklore and genre?
9. Rise in popularity and decline in popularity of genres. Why did the western disappear in America? Why are soap operas invading prime-time? What genres are dominant and what does this dominance reflect about American society and culture?
10. Differences in genres in different media. Are differences to be found, for example, in mysteries made for television and mysteries made for film? If so, what significance might these differences have?
11. What uses and gratifications do different genres provide for audiences? How do people *use* genres? Do different genres provide different gratifications for different groups? If so, what groups like which genres and why?
12. How do technical matters involving production and aesthetics impact on different genres? For example, situation comedies and action adventure films tend to be shot in different ways, have different kinds of lighting, and so forth. What impact do these matters have?
13. How does one deal with genres best? Do we focus upon representative texts or do we focus on stylistic and other aspects of genres, and cite examples from texts at appropriate points?

It is possible and desirable to deal with a number of these considerations at the same time. I have listed a number of approaches that genre critics might use in analyzing and interpreting texts and genres; I have not meant to suggest that we should limit ourselves to any one of them, though we might, in certain cases, wish to focus on one or two of them.

Genre criticism represents an attempt by analysts and interpreters of texts to have the best of both worlds—to be structuralists and formalists (in dealing with the structural elements in texts and formulaic aspects of texts) and to be culture critics (in dealing with the relationships that exist between the texts and the culture and societies in which they are found). The matter becomes even more complicated as mixed genres develop. We find genres borrowing from and blending into other genres. For example, news programs use dramatic simulations and soap operas (such as *Twin Peaks*) merge with horror stories (and adopt filmic cinematic conventions). MTV blends avant garde film techniques, including intertextual quotations in places, into performances that function as commercials. One could go on, endlessly here.

Artistic texts, we now realize, are extremely complicated phenomena. We have good reason to believe that those who create these texts are not fully conscious of all that they are doing and that we who read, watch, and listen to these texts are not aware of how they affect us, as individuals, and society in general. Dealing with them in their awesome complexity—in terms of text, genre and context—is a difficult task but a fascinating and important one.

The highest expression of this aestheticizing tendency is in George Stevens' *Shane*, where the legend of the West is virtually reduced to its essentials and then fixed in the dreamy clarity of a fairy tale. There never was so broad and bare and lovely a landscape as Stevens puts before us, or so unimaginably comfortless a "town" as the little group of buildings on the prairie to which the settlers must come for their supplies and to buy a drink. . . . The hero (Alan Ladd) is hardly a man at all, but something like the Spirit of the West, beautiful in fringed buckskins. He emerges mysteriously from the plains, breathing sweetness and a melancholy which is no longer simply the Westerner's natural response to experience but has taken on spirituality; and when he has accomplished his mission, meeting and destroying in the black figure of Jack Palance a Spirit of Evil just as metaphysical as his own embodiment of virtue, he fades away again into the more distant West, a man whose "day is over," leaving behind the wondering little boy who might have imagined the whole story.

SOURCE: Warshow, R. (1964, p. 102). *The Immediate Experience*. New York: Anchor Books.

5

Genre, Society, and Culture

This chapter deals with a number of social and political aspects of genre. It begins with a discussion of the four political cultures that exist in America (according to the theories of Aaron Wildavsky, a prominent political scientist at the University of California) and with speculations about which genres might appeal to these political cultures. It then discusses the relationship between genres and the life cycle and suggests that as we get older we engage in "genre migration," moving, for example, from listening to hard rock radio stations when we are adolescents to easy listening radio stations when we are middle aged.

The chapter also includes a discussion of the impact of dramatic fictions on television, on people, and how people become addicted to television. After that, it offers a list of common uses and gratifications supplied by television and suggests how various genres may relate to the various uses and gratifications. Next, it compares the way crime shows and situation comedies are made and concludes with a discussion of the evolution of the western and how westerns reflect political values.

Strength of Group Boundaries

		weak	strong
	many	fatalists	elitists
Number and Variety of Prescriptions	few	individualists	egalitarians

Figure 5.1. Model of four political cultures. Adapted from M. Douglas and A. Wildavsky, 1982; see Wildavsky, 1986.

Genres and Politics

For my point of departure in this discussion of genres and politics, I will take Aaron Wildavsky's suggestion that in all societies there are four political cultures: hierarchical elitists, individualists, egalitarians and fatalists. These groups are defined as follows:

> *Hierarchial elitists* justify inequality, show deference to superiors, value of order, sacrifice parts for the whole.
>
> *Individualists* believe freedom of contract is basic, that humans are self-seeking, that government should protect property, and defend the country.
>
> *Egalitarians* stress equality of needs, criticize hierarchy and individualism, which form the "establishment."
>
> *Fatalists* see life as based on chance, luck.

Wildavsky argues that two dominant questions arise in any cultural theory—"who am I?" (that is, what group do I belong to?) and "how should I behave?" (that is, what rules should I obey?). By setting up a four-celled figure that considers group boundaries and the number and variety of prescriptions in a culture, he arrives at these political cultures.[1]

The question of interest is: Can Wildavsky's schema be used to understand the appeal of certain genres? And more precisely, would certain political cultures, by view of their values and beliefs, tend to be more interested in some genres than others? I assume

Hierarchical Elitists	*Competitive Individualists*
News (International)	Sports
Classical mysteries	Westerns
Spy stories	Mysteries (Private eyes)
Egalitarians	*Fatalists*
Stand up comedies	Soaps
Zany comedies (Monty Python)	Country western music

Figure 5.2. Political culture and genre preference.

that people watch television programs, go to films, and read books that support and reinforce their values and beliefs and avoid texts that challenge these beliefs. Let us assume, for argument's sake, that we have readers and viewers of texts who like the genres they should like. What might we find? This exercise is highly speculative, of course, but it does yield some interesting results.

I assigned international news to the hierarchical elitists because these programs tend to be about the comings and goings of the various elites who run countries and make decisions of national and international importance. Elitists would also like the classical mysteries because they tend to be about elites—the classical English ones often involve aristocratic types who live in large mansions with servants, family members who lust after inheritances, and so forth. Elitists would also be drawn to spy stories because they frequently involve the adventures of elite figures (or pseudo-elite figures, like James Bond, who likes his drinks shaken but not stirred and has other seemingly aristocratic tastes).

Competitive Individualists, I would argue, should be drawn to sports contests—especially ones like tennis and golf that involve individuals competing with other individuals. Were westerns still popular, individualists would be drawn to them, in that many feature the lone cowboy who single-handedly cleans up a corrupt town and vanquishes evil. And, of course, competitive individualists would follow the adventures of "private eyes," detectives who solve crimes and find murderers, generally competing with and outwitting the police (who are often shown as inept and frequently hinder the private eye).

For the Egalitarians, the most significant genre would be comedies—especially the kind like *Monty Python* that ridicule society and its institutions (and various elements in society, as well, such as the hierarchical elitists found in government, the church, etc.). Humor can be a means of resistance to the powerful elements in society who control the media and run the government. Humor is generally a liberating force, an antiestablishment force (though it can also be used by the elites for their purposes).

As M. M. Bakhtin (1981), a Russian literary theorist, explains in *The Dialogic Imagination*:

> It is precisely laughter that destroys the epic, and in general destroys any hierarchical (distancing and valorized) distance. As a distanced image a subject cannot be comical; to be made comical, it must be brought close. Everything that makes us laugh is close at hand, all comical creativity works in the zone of maximal proximity.... Laughter demolishes fear and piety before an object, before a world, making it an object of familiar contact and thus clearing the ground for an absolutely free investigation of it. Laughter is a vital factor in laying down that prerequisite for fearlessness without which it would be impossible to approach the world realistically. (p. 23)

What Bakhtin points out is that humor is, by its very nature, a subversive force and one that destroys the sense of solemnity and distance that those we have called hierarchical elitists use to justify inequality. Humor enables people to see things realistically, by bringing things "close" and enabling people to inspect them.

The kind of comedy that egalitarians would logically like would be that found in the better stand-up comedians, which often deal with the fiascos and absurdity of political life and comedy shows that have a satirical or absurdist aspect to them.

Finally, for the fatalists, if we follow the logic of their beliefs and values, we end up with country and western songs, which often deal with the trials and tribulations of common people who find themselves fired from their jobs, deserted by their loved ones, and so on. These motifs are also found in soap operas, which deal with the same kinds of things, though generally they involve middle- and upper-class characters who tend to be professional, businessmen and women. Soap operas are complex texts that offer gratifications to all of the political cultures, though logically they should be of most interest to the fatalists, who can identify with the problems the characters in soaps face and perhaps aspire to the kinds of lifestyles they lead.

Logically, fatalists should not watch films or television programs that show that one can succeed on the basis of individual initiative, that show that society functions because of the doings of elitists (who have a sense of obligation to those beneath them, unlike the competitive individualists), or that stress the things that everyone has in common rather than the things on which they differ. Whether fatalists or any of the political cultures consume the genres they *should* consume is a difficult question. Because texts are so complex, they often offer gratifications that make them of interest to members of political cultures that on the basis of pure logic should not be attracted to them.

Although this discussion is highly speculative and based on people in the political cultures acting according to the logic of their beliefs, it is possible to survey people and find out whether members of the different political cultures actually are attracted to certain genres and find others distasteful. This would reveal whether there is, in fact, a relationship between political cultures and preferences for various genres and kinds of popular culture.

Marxists, who are egalitarians, argue that the media and popular culture are instruments of ideological domination by the ruling classes, the classes that own the modes of production in any given society. Their focus tends to be on the way particular works or important mass media heroes and heroines spread ideological messages. But they are also concerned about the ideological aspects of various genres, even though they regard genres as hard to classify according to their ideological implications.

Thus in Bennett and Woollacott's (1987) *Bond and Beyond* there is a discussion of the ideological implications of genres.

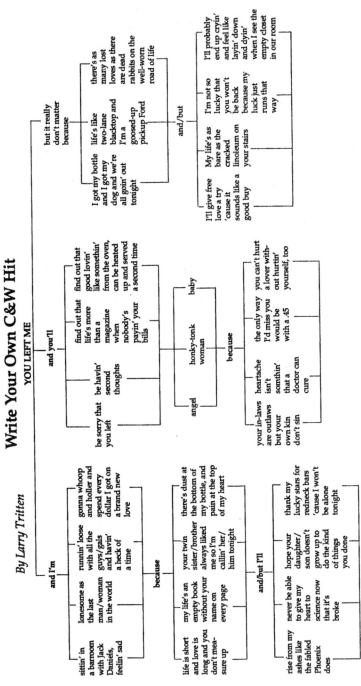

Figure 5.3. Formula for country and western song. Published by permission of Larry Tritten. © Larry Tritten.

> The discourses which are worked across in the western, the gangster
> film and the detective film are . . . substantially the same: discourses
> concerning crime, the law, justice, social order, and so on. (p. 96)

These areas are connected to the political order, obviously. Our
attitudes toward the law, the justice system, and the social order
affect our political values.

In the case of Bond, our authors suggest, the Bond novels do not
merely carry simple ideological messages or deal with tensions
between competing ideologies. What they do is dramatize situations, creating crises which, they assert, relocate the ideologies of
Bond's readers and viewers. This would suggest that narrative
techniques and structures have ideological dimensions to them,
and ideological messages are transmitted not only through content
(Bond as a symbol of NATO, Englishness, etc.) but also through the
form the Bond novels and films take.

How one demonstrates the assertion that readers and audiences
actually are "relocated" ideologically is another matter. The notion
has implications for those interested in the relationship that exists
between genres and ideology.

Genres and the Life Cycle

In 1984-1985 I was a visiting professor at the Annenberg School
for Communication at the University of Southern California. I
taught a course on popular culture. One week I brought in the
vice-president of what we would call an "easy listening" station to
talk about the radio industry. When I introduced the speaker and
mentioned the station he came from, the students all laughed.
"That's okay," said the speaker. "Laugh. What's really going to be
funny is that when you are thirty-five and forty, you'll all be
listening to my station. I'll have the last laugh." What this little
story suggests is that when we listen to the radio (and stations tend
to be genre-specific) and when we watch television, read books,
and so forth we often move from genre to genre as we move
through the life cycle. This genre migration does not mean that we

always abandon other genres, but in some cases we seem to derive more pleasure from one genre than from others. This is probably because different genres speak to different needs we have.

Genre Migrations and the Life Cycle

It is difficult to determine with any precision the way people migrate from genre to genre as they get older. As far as radio is concerned, if our informant is to be believed, it is quite reasonable to assume that as we get older, our tastes may change somewhat, and we migrate from the rock music of our teens to soft and easy music in our thirties and forties, as well as news and talk shows. Research indicates that the audiences of talk shows tend to be made up of people over fifty.

Let me offer a highly speculative table on genres and the life cycle, based on discussions with child librarians, radio broadcasters, and others in the media.

There is a logic to our interest in specific genres (which will be discussed in more detail in the section on uses and gratifications). As we get older and move through the life cycle, we face certain psychological challenges that we need to deal with and, presumably, different genres help us deal with specific problems. We are not conscious, I would add, of the problems we face or of the forces leading us to the different genres, but just as children need fairy tales when they are around five years old, and for a few years or so after that, so do adolescents need the kinds of music they listen to and the kinds of stories they are drawn to in books (for those who read books), on television and in the movies.

There is a problem involving genres and the life cycle, as it is involved in television viewing, that I would like to discuss. In a number of cases there is reason to believe that children are watching programs from genres that are not appropriate to their emotional development, leading to what I describe as a "vicious cycle," and this viewing has a significant impact on their lives.

TABLE 5.1 Genres and Stages in the Life Cycle

Stage in Life Cycle	Genre of Interest
Babies	Lullabies
Children (5 to 7)	Fairy tales
Early teens	Love, adventure, mystery
Teenagers	Science fiction, sports
Young adults, adults	News, sports, soaps, cops, etc.
Middle aged	News, soaps, etc.
Senior citizens	News, talk shows, obituaries

Vicious Cycles: Inappropriate Genres and Television Viewing

In *A Psychiatric Study of Myths and Fairy Tales*, Dr. Julius E. Heuscher (1974) discusses the problems caused when young children read or watch stories that involve matters beyond their emotional levels. He writes that

> all through the previous chapters we have seen how folklore stresses the need for a harmonious, gradual human development; how growing up cannot be rushed without serious consequences to the spiritual aspects of the human being. The child who is being presented with an overabundance of adult-life conflicts and desires, and who thereby is being pushed toward grown-up ideas, tends to become afraid of growing up and is therefore stunted in his maturation process. (p. 325)

Young children generally do not read novels and short stories that are not appropriate for them because of the difficulty of reading this material. But they watch programs on television that are not appropriate for them and, if Heuscher is correct, suffer from their exposure to this material. This leads to what I describe as a "vicious cycle" generated by viewing inappropriate texts and genres on television.

    a. Viewing inappropriate genres (for example, soap operas, full of adult conflicts) on television by children leads to fear of growing up and

      becoming an adult, because that means being involved with trou-
bling conflicts.

  b. This fear of growing up and becoming an adult leads to an unconscious fear of sustained emotional relationships and commitments.

  c. This fear of sustained relationships leads, in turn, to fear of marriage,
to nonrelational sex, and to a fear of emotions in general.

  d. The people affected by these fears are unhappy and lead unsatisfying
lives, engendering anxiety, misery, escapism (via drugs and other
means, such as television) as a means of obtaining relief.

  e. Television viewing becomes, then, a narcotic upon which people
become dependent, to assuage their loneliness. But at the same time
that television programs (and genres) provide relief, they also re-
awaken and reinforce our childhood fears, by presenting viewers
with characters involved in serious conflicts, who may be violent,
who are often unhappy and face numerous problems (especially on
soap operas) which viewers relied on television to escape from in the
first place.

  f. Thus television creates the very dependencies that people try to
overcome by watching it and people become prisoners of their
television sets . . . and, in effect, prisoners of themselves.

We now recognize that there are people who are addicted to
television, who watch enormous amounts of it—sometimes as
much as 70 or 100 hours per week. But even ordinary Americans,
who are not addicts, watch an average of more than three and a
half hours per day, so most of us might be described as mildly
addicted to television.

Television is often blamed for many of the ills we face in society;
obviously other factors need to be considered. But when it comes
to the emotional problems many young people face (such as a
desire to lead emotion free lives and lack of impulse control), I think
television bears a great deal of responsibility. When we talk about
television, I might add, we are not generally talking about the
technical aspects of the medium but about the programs it carries
and ultimately, for our purposes, about the genres these programs
fall under.

Let us now move to a related consideration, the uses and gratifications people obtain by watching different television (and film)

TABLE 5.2 Media, Genres, and Uses and Gratifications

Mass media	Radio, television, film, books, magazines, newspapers, records, etc.
Selected genres	News, soap operas, commercials, documentaries, talk shows, detective stories, sports, science fiction stories, spy stories, etc.
Uses and gratifications	Be amused, see authority figures exalted, experience the beautiful, gain an identity, see villains in action, see order imposed on the world, gain common frame of reference, etc.

genres. The same, of course, applies to literary works, but we do not, on the average, read novels for three and a half hours each day.

The Uses of Media

The theory of uses and gratifications was developed in the 1960s and focused on the uses people made of media and the various gratifications the media provided for people. This perspective did not ask "what does media and the texts they carry do to people" but "why do people choose this or that kind of programming?" It is assumed that people choose certain texts on the basis of needs they have and gratifications they seek, and thus are active participants in the communication process. From our perspective, of course, it is not the medium but the genre that is of major significance. This is because media carry (though they also affect) texts (or kinds of programs in the case of radio and television) and texts within a genre tend to be formulaic. The genre is found in between the medium of transmission and the specific text and provides a way of seeing how texts might be used and the kinds of gratifications they provide. Table 5.2 illustrates this relationship.

The media transmit individual works (specific films, songs, television shows, books) but as I have pointed out earlier we have learned to think about these works in terms of their genres: this

TABLE 5.3 Uses and Gratifications and Appropriate Genres

Selected Uses and Gratifications of Media	Appropriate Genres
1. Be amused	Sitcoms, comedies
2. See authority figures exalted, deflated	News, comedies
3. Experience the beautiful	Travel, love stories
4. Obtain a common frame of reference	Media events
5. Satisfy curiosity, be informed	Science, soap operas
6. Identify with deity, divine powers	Science fiction
7. Find distraction and diversion	Sports, soaps
8. Experience empathy	Soaps
9. Have strong, guilt free emotions	Soaps, cops
10. Find models to imitate	Soaps, sports
11. Gain an identity	Commercials, soaps
12. Reinforce belief in justice	Cops, mysteries
13. Experience romantic love	Soaps
14. See magic, marvels, the miraculous	Science fiction
15. See others make mistakes	Sports, news
16. See order imposed on the world	Science, news
17. Participate in history	Media events
18. Be purged of powerful emotions	Soaps, cops
19. Find vicarious outlet for sexual drives	Soaps
20. Explore taboo subjects with impunity	Soaps
21. Experience the ugly, grotesque	Science fiction
22. See moral, cultural values upheld	Sports
23. See villains in action	Spy, crime, mysteries

program is a sitcom, that film is a horror flick, and so on. That is because, in part, the identity of a text is connected to its genre.

Let me now list (Table 5.3) some of the more important uses people make of the mass media and gratifications the media provide and suggest some of the genres that are most appropriate to a given use or gratification. In some cases, I have used what might be described as subgenres in this table, but I think it shows how various genres relate to needs and gratifications people have. Media events (Academy Awards, visits by the pope, the Super Bowl, etc.) might come under news and, in certain cases, sports or some other genre, depending on how specific we wish to be.

The point I have tried to make, however, is that it is to genres we should turn (ultimately) when we wish to see how people use a given text such as *Dallas* or *Alien* or *Murder on the Orient Express* or the Superbowl.

Crime Shows and Situation
Comedies on Television

Although crime shows and situation comedies both are popular genres on television, there are a number of differences between the two genres that have social and political dimensions. In an article "TV-Formulas: Prime-Time Glue," Joyce Nelson (1979) compares these two genres.[2]

Table 5.4, based on a chart Nelson uses in her essay, shows the differences between the two formulas—the two dominant genres—in 1979, when she wrote her article, as well as in the 1990s, though there have been some changes in both formulas in recent years. She points out that crime shows tend to have last names of heroes (*Kojak, Mannix, Baretta*) that convey authority while sitcoms have first names (*Julia, Rhoda, Laverne and Shirley*) that convey informality and lack of power.

The crime shows are shot on film, which she suggests, provides crisper, harder-edged images with more depth, and the action takes place on the Z-axis, namely toward and away from the camera. This creates a sense of urgency as the action moves toward and away from viewers. On the other hand, situation comedies are generally shot on videotape, which gives a fuzzier and flatter image. And the action is generally confined to sets of interiors of houses; there is little dramatic action, with the focus being, instead, on close-up shots of facial expressions, small gestures and somewhat restricted body movements.

Sitcoms, which are generally taped before live audiences, have a good deal of dialogue (and use laugh tracks) whereas crime shows are oriented more toward action and more rapid-paced cutting from scene to scene. This editing, I might add, also contributes to a heightened sense of excitement in viewers, who are forced to keep up with the rapid moving events in the story. The other oppositions

TABLE 5.4 Crime Show and Sitcom Formulas

Crime Show formula.	Situation Comedy Formula
Film	Videotape
Images sharp, in depth	Images soft, flat
Large scale movement	Confined movement
Action centered	Dialogue centered
Musical track	Laugh track
Public, urban setting	Private, interior setting
Work oriented	Leisure oriented
Loners	Groups
Wise, effective authority figures	Bumbling, ineffective commoners
Hour long	Half hour long
Titles: last names	Titles: first names
Uncompromising winners	Compromising, vulnerable losers
Formal, heroic	Informal, unheroic
Like network news	Like celebrity talk shows

listed in the chart more or less speak for themselves. The major figures in situation comedies are what Nelson calls "lovable losers" who are shown, generally, at leisure (getting excited about all kinds of trivial events) while the major figures in the crime shows are heroic figures who are shown at work, facing challenges, triumphing over them, and helping to keep society functioning.

These two formulas, Nelson adds, resemble two other important television genres—network news programs and talk shows. Network news shows involve "politicians or leaders involved in the ritualistic display of authority" while talk shows are full of celebrities gossiping about their personal lives, being funny (Berger 1988, p. 192).

Ultimately, Nelson argues, these two formulas work for the benefit of advertisers. She writes that

> a curious ideology arises from the formulas of the sitcom and crime series in combination. Wisdom, authority, decisive action, and leadership qualities are rarely associated with the characters who most closely resemble us in our living rooms. Instead, those qualities are reserved for people who are set apart: the law enforcers and event-explainers, a small group of authority figures who nightly re-enact their expertise. As well, the outside world, the world beyond the

confines of the home, seems one of danger, crime, disaster and complexity that only a few can cope with. The majority must bumble through their small, daily frustrations and personal problems, never questioning or mentioning the bigger events, the larger forces at work in society. (Berger, 1991, pp. 192, 193)

In this context, Nelson argues, the products advertised on television are shown as the one area in which we can make reasoned, intelligent choices and that the one role offered to us is that of good consumers. "On commercial prime time," she adds "our wisdom is supposed to be product knowledge and our leadership qualities are to be shown in fervent brand loyalty, daring attempts to squeeze the toilet paper or even the great good fortune of writing our own commercials for a laundry detergent" (Berger, 1991, p. 193).

Genres, then, have social implications and social consequences. They offer us roles to imitate and generate world views that shape our social and political behavior. The development of the thirty second political commercial and its all-consuming importance in campaigns makes this quite evident. As particular genres evolve, they also generate and reinforce certain values and beliefs, a matter which I would like to discuss next, by examining the evolution of the western.

Sixguns and Society: A Structuralist-Ideological Analysis

Structuralism, for our purposes, will be defined as a method of analysis that interprets texts in terms of the relationships that exist among the basic elements found in a text. What structuralism is and is not is a subject of considerable debate. Robert Scholes (1974) writes that

at the heart of the idea of structuralism is the idea of system: a complete, self-regulating entity that adapts to new conditions by transforming its features while retaining its systematic structure. Every literary unit, from the individual sentence to the whole order of words can be seen in relation to the concept of system. In particular, we look at individual works, literary genres, and the whole of literature as related systems, and at literature as a system within the larger system of human culture. (p. 10)

Structuralists see texts (and I am simplifying things here, admittedly) as systems in which the way units relate to one another generates meaning. For example, the order of the words in a sentence affects the meaning of the sentence.

This notion that relationships are crucial in generating meaning was found in Saussure, who pointed out that concepts "are purely differential" and derive their meaning "not from their positive content" but from their relationship to the other terms in the system. "The most precise characteristics" of concepts, he adds, "is in being what the others are not" (Saussure, 1966, p. 117). We might call this the Seven-Up Un-cola theory of concepts.

When we apply structuralist notions to texts, we use Saussure's insight about the meaning of concepts being based on a relationship of opposition to other concepts and apply this to characters and events. (This is an adaptation of the ideas of the French anthropologist, Claude Lévi-Strauss, who elicited patterns of opposition in myths.) As Jonathan Culler (1975), a semiotician has written, "Structuralists have generally followed Jakobson and taken the binary opposition as a fundamental operation of the human mind basic to the production of meaning" (p. 15). So, when we make a structuralist analysis, we look for patterns: relationships among characters, kinds of plots, and that kind of thing.

Sixguns and Society is a book (Wright, 1975) that is a structural study of the western. What Wright argues is that as the western evolved, it reflected basic changes in American society, as it moved from laissez-faire economics in the 1930s to modern corporate capitalism.

Wright makes a structural analysis of westerns and suggests that there are four basic plots found in them—what we might call four subgenres. These plots and their characteristics are shown in Table 5.5, which I have elicited from his book. Wright lists the top grossing westerns for every year between 1931 and 1972 and

TABLE 5.5 Basic Plots in Westerns

Period	Name of Plot	Characteristic of Plot
1930-1955	Classical	Lone gunfighter who saves town or farmers from gamblers or ranchers
1950-1960	Vengeance	Ill-used hero finds no justice in society, becomes gunfighter seeking vengeance
Early 1950s	Transition	Hero and heroine defend justice but are rejected by society
1958-1970	Professional	Heroes are professional fighters who take jobs for money

identifies them according to his classification scheme. In the book he discusses important examples of each plot variation. Examples of these variations are shown in Table 5.6.

Wright discusses each of these films and uses Propp's (1968) morphology to deal with the structural characteristics of each variation.

The conclusion he reaches, in his chapter on "Myth and Meaning" is particularly interesting. He suggests that it is "through the narrative action that the conceptual symbolism of the Western, or any myth, is understood and applied by its hearers (or viewers)" (1975, p. 186). He then summarizes the messages found in the westerns he has analyzed.

> In the Western, the classical plot shows that the way to achieve such human rewards as friendship, respect, and dignity is to separate yourself from others and use your strength as an autonomous individual to succor them. This plot exists in the context of a restricted but active market economy. The vengeance variation—in the context of a tentative planned economy—weakens the compatibility of the individual and society by showing that the path to respect and love

TABLE 5.6 Examples of Western Plot Variations

Western Subgenre	Movie Examples
Classical	*Shane* *Dodge City* *Canyon Passage* *Duel in the Sun* *The Far Country*
Vengeance	*Stagecoach* *The Man from Laramie* *One-Eyed Jacks* *Nevada Smith*
Transition Theme	*High Noon* *Broken Arrow* *Johnny Guitar*
Professional	*Rio Bravo* *The Professionals* *The Wild Bunch* *Butch Cassidy and the Sundance Kid*

is to separate yourself from others, struggling individually against your many and strong enemies but striving to remember and return to the softer values of marriage and humility. The transition theme, anticipating new social values, argues that love and companionship are available—at the cost of becoming a social outcast—to the individual who stands firmly and righteously against the intolerance and ignorance of society. Finally, the professional plot—in the context of a corporate economy—argues that companionship and respect are to be achieved only by becoming a skilled technician, who joins an elite group of professionals, accepts any job that is offered, and has loyalty only to the integrity of the team, not to any competing social or community values. (1975, pp. 186, 187)

What this all adds up to, Wright argues, is that westerns offer models that describe the way we are supposed to be and act and these models have to be seen in the context of (and as reflections of) economic institutions and the values and belief structures that they generate. It is on the narrative level we must focus our attention, remembering that every event in these stories is connected to the success or failure of the protagonists and that these must be interpreted as such.

Meaning, Wright tells us, only exists as the result of interpretation and interpretations cannot be "proved" false or correct. You have to see whether the given interpretation makes sense of the events in the story. At the same time, as Wright has tried to show, stories tend to reflect changes going on in the economic and political structure of society: the westerns evolved, mirroring changes taking place in the American economic system. This mirroring is, of course, not done consciously by writers of westerns or anyone involved in producing them. The changes in the westerns reflect changes in American society as felt by writers, who then, without consciously trying to do so (generally speaking, that is) mirrored these changes in their scripts.

Formulaic stories, then, have social significance both as individual stories and as examples of genres and both must be considered when dealing with the social, cultural, and political significance of texts or genres. We cannot forget about texts in dealing with genres nor can we forget about genres when dealing with texts.

In the chapters that follow, I will examine the classical mystery genre and five classic texts, each of which was chosen as a representative example of a genre. These case studies deal with the texts but also with the genres they represent and the social and political implications of both the work and its genres in many cases. This, I would suggest, is the way we should deal with texts—with the work itself, with its genre and with the social and cultural dimensions of the text and its genre.

I have selected texts that I consider to be historically important representatives of their genres and excellent works of art, as well. (For those who argue that genre fiction is never excellent, let me substitute the word "interesting.") All of these texts are novels that have been made into films and one, *War of the Worlds*, was a historically important radio program, as well.

I wanted to use novels because they are all easily obtainable and, because they are in the print medium, relatively easy to work with (in contrast, say, to a film or television show). The printed word, as

they say, "lives." It is possible to consider the way these novels have
been made into films and thus deal with the relationship that exists
between media and genres, as well.

Notes

1. This figure is adapted from work by Mary Douglas in the book *Risk and
Culture* by Douglas and Wildavsky (1982). For a more detailed examination of
Wildavsky's theories, see A. A. Berger (1990), *Agitpop: Political Culture and Communication Theory.*
2. This article originally appeared in the Canadian publication *In Search* in 1979
and was reprinted in A. A. Berger (1991).

As we see now, Poe's criminological yarns show a concern for the way in which scientific method, especially in psychology and secondarily in sociology, begins to assert itself as a mode of social control. The ratiocinative genius of the gentleman specialist is necessary, in the new urban and industrial order, to pierce the web of criminal circumstance. Criminals are defined as superindividuals let loose in an anomic society; they can be caught up with only by a Cartesian mentality that can identify with the "mechanisms" of their aberrant humanity. Deviance is fundamentally systemic—"Vice and virtue are products like vitriol and sugar," Taine said—and it can be controlled not by feudal bailiffs and sheriffs, but by men wise in the ways of modernity.

SOURCE: Denney, R. (1989, p. 201) *The Astonished Muse*. New Brunswick, NJ: Transaction Books.

6

The Classic Mystery: A Case Study

Historical Roots of the Mystery

There is general agreement among scholars that the detective mystery story, with a fictional character solving a mystery by using logic and deductive reasoning, began with Edgar Allan Poe's story "The Murders in the Rue Morgue." It was published in April of 1841. Poe created a character, C. August Dupin, who has been described by Ellery Queen as "the world's first fictional detective in the modern sense" (Loundes, 1970). Poe wrote two other stories featuring Dupin—"The Mystery of Marie Rôget" and "The Purloined Letter."

In these stories Poe established many of the conventions of the modern classic mystery story. For one thing, his protagonist, C. August Dupin, is somewhat eccentric, thus serving as the prototype for legions of other detectives who have various curious (in some cases even bizarre) personality traits. These personality traits fascinate us and contribute to our interest in the stories.

This matter of having heroes with strange tastes may be a reflection of attitudes we have about intellectuals and others who use their minds and are in possession of arcane knowledge; it is a kind of romantic notion, similar to those we have about artists and creative people. As a representative example of the strange detective, consider Nero Wolfe, who is an enormously fat man who never leaves his house, cultivates orchards and is excessively interested in food. He also is brilliant and solves mysteries that mystify the police and everyone else. Sherlock Holmes also has his curious traits and interests—and the same could be said about many other classical detectives, such as Hercules Poirot, Miss Marples, and so forth.

The Three Dominant Kinds
of Mysteries

Since Poe's creations, the murder mystery has evolved and been modified. In addition to detectives such as C. August Dupin, we now have tough-guy detectives such as Sam Spade, who are "private eyes," and we have detectives such as Dick Tracy (in the comics) who are members of police forces and are involved in what are often called police procedurals. Although all three detectives use their brains to solve crimes, there are some differences worth noting. These differences are illustrated in Table 6.1.

Table 6.1 presents an "ideal-type." There are so many mysteries that have been written in books, for radio, television, and film, that it is impossible to cover everything or make ironclad generalities, but I think we can see that there are considerable differences among the three different kinds of mysteries.

The classical detective is not involved with a bureaucracy and with technology (reports by pathologists about the contents of the stomachs of those murdered, etc.) but uses his (or her) intellectual resources to solve the crime—which almost invariably is a murder. The classical detective often helps the police, who are confounded and frequently focus their attention on the wrong suspect.

Now that we have differentiated the classical mystery from other kinds of mysteries (the hero of these stories often is not a detective, but has an interest in crime and talent for solving crimes—like Jane Marples), let us consider some of the other attributes of the classical mystery.

TABLE 6.1 Three Basic Detective Types

Categories	Classical	Tough Guy	Procedural
Occupation	Private citizen	Private eye	Police official
Personality	Eccentric	Cynic/worldly	Cynic/bureaucratic
Skills	Logic, mind	Tough, smart	Technology, brains
Story ambience	Wealthy	All classes	All classes
Hero in danger	Never	Always	Sometimes
Location	Great house	Urban	Urban

Tzvetan Todorov's Typology

Tzvetan Todorov (1973), a Bulgarian born critic now living in Paris, has written a good deal on genres.[1] He points out that one reason we avoid writing about genres is that to identify a work as being part of a genre is to devalue it. This, he suggests, stems from a reaction against the classical period, which was more interested in genres than individual works and not only described genres, but prescribed them.

In Todorov's (1988) typology there are three kinds of mysteries. The first is what he calls "the whodunit," the classic works which reached their peak of popularity between the two world wars. These whodunits contain, he suggests, two stories—the crime and the investigation. The first story, the crime, tells what happened and the second story, the investigation, tells how we know about it. And it is the second story, the investigation, Todorov argues, that dominates and excites our interest.

The second kind of mystery for Todorov is "the thriller," which he says was created in the United States around the time of the Second World War. In thrillers, the two stories are fused—the first story is suppressed and the second story, the investigation, is vitalized. Todorov (1988) writes "Rules for Writing a Classic Mystery (A Whodunit)":

> We are no longer told about a crime anterior to the moment of the narrative; the narrative coincides with the action. No thriller is presented in the form of memoirs: there is no point reached where the

narrator comprehends all past events, we do not even know if he will
reach the end of the story alive. Prospection takes the place of intro-
spection.

There is no story to be guessed; and there is no mystery, in the sense
that it was present in the whodunit. But the reader's interest is not
thereby diminished; we realize here that two entirely different forms
of interest exist. The first can be called *curiosity*; it proceeds from effect
to cause: starting from a certain effect (a corpse and certain clues) we
must find its cause (the culprit and his motive). The second form is
suspense, and here the movement is from cause to effect: we are first
shown the causes . . . and our interest is sustained by the expectation
of what will happen. (p. 161)

I think Todorov is wrong in arguing that the hero of the thriller
never is able to make sense of things at the end of the story. But
Todorov does focus our attention on the importance of action and
suspense in thrillers. He also points out that some authors, such as
Dashiell Hammett and Raymond Chandler do not suppress the
mystery part of their thrillers (or what I would describe as tough
guy detective stories).

Todorov's third category, the "suspense novel," combines the
properties of the whodunit and the thriller. It keeps the mystery
element of the whodunit though it focuses attention on the second
story, the investigation, but it does not reduce this investigation to
a simple matter of discovering the truth. The reader is interested in
both what happened in the past and what is happening in the
present. Todorov suggests that Hammett and Chandler wrote suspense novels—stories in which the detective, a private eye, was
often beaten up, threatened with death, may have had a love
interest, and was continually risking his life. He is no longer an
independent observer of things, the way the classical detective is,
but is integrated into the world of the other characters. This detective is what I have called the "tough guy" detective, the private eye,
in my typology.

Todorov sees this suspense novel as serving as a transition
between the classic detective novel and the thriller but as he points
out, some authors have written several different kinds of mysteries
and in some cases it is impossible to classify a given novel as
belonging to any of his three categories. New genres, he suggests,

are always being born—not by negating previous ones but by taking some aspects of other genres and making them dominant. I find Todorov's names for his categories somewhat misleading. I have no problem with the classic detective mysteries being called whodunits; these mysteries are often known by that term. Generally speaking, we call the works of Hammett and Chandler detective stories featuring tough guy or hard boiled detectives. There is, of course, suspense in these stories, in that we do not know whether the hero will survive, let alone find the villain or villains—but suspense can be found in all kinds of other genres as well. I would make the same comment about his term *thrillers*. Some scholars have used that term to describe spy stories and other genres as well.

But Todorov does perform a useful service to us in pointing out how mysteries are really composed of two stories, the crime and the investigation, and different kinds of mysteries focus attention on these elements in different ways.

Attributes of the Classical Detective Story

In the book *The Mystery Writer's Art*, edited by Francis M. J. Nevins, Jr. (1970), there is an article that deals with a number of the attributes of what we are calling the classic detective mystery. Robert A. W. Lowndes' (1970) "The Contributions of Edgar Allen Poe," lists many of the rules for writing classical mysteries that are found in (and stem from) "The Murders in the Rue Morgue." The list that follows is an adaptation and selection I have made of these rules, with some of my own notions added.

1. The detective is a private citizen and never was a member of a police organization. He has an interest in crime and frequently, by chance, finds himself on the scene of a murder and becomes involved in figuring out who did it.
2. The detectives are eccentric—to varying degrees. They have to interest and intrigue us, somehow, as individuals and we have to feel positive about them—perhaps even identify with them. The other characters must be of interest, also. In the classic mysteries, the characters are often very wealthy and live in grand homes or large

estates whose architectural features sometimes (especially in locked room murders) play an important role in things. There are many servants and so forth and all kinds of hatreds and jealousies among the members of the family or household, many of whom have personality disorders and deficiencies. Thus, there are many possible suspects on hand who might have murdered the victim. In many cases, the plot also involves preventing the second murder before it happens—or trying to prevent it—as well as discovering who the murderer is.

3. The detective is often seen through the eyes of a companion and his exploits are revealed by this companion. The classic case: Dr. Watson and Sherlock Holmes.

4. Clues are presented that the reader does not recognize but which the detective does recognize. Detectives often know a great deal of information about all kinds of arcane subjects and also have great insight into psychology and human motivation. In the language of semiotics, we would say that readers/viewers are presented with signifiers that they dismiss or do not decode correctly. We find many clues in descriptive passages, to which most readers pay little attention. The reader of the classic detective mystery invariably is in competition with the detective to interpret the clues and solve the crime before the detective identifies the criminal. These clues should, if they are all interpreted properly, give us a pretty good idea of who the criminal is—though there still may be questions because we generally miss some important clues or make incorrect inferences about them.

5. Even when the reader does recognize the most important clues, the mystery still can seem impossible. This is often the case with locked room mysteries in which readers and viewers who are competing with the detective do not put things together correctly.

6. The detective sometimes sets a trap for the criminal and thus exposes the criminal in some final *dénouement*. This is often done in cases in which there is not enough evidence to prove that someone is the murderer even though the detective knows who did it.

7. The police generally suspect the wrong person or persons. They generally need the assistance of the hero and often have a hostile (to varying degrees) relationship with him or her. Often there are reasons for suspecting all of the main characters. There is a rule that needs explanation: the butler never does it. This means the killer has to be one of the main characters in the story and has to have good reason—psychological problems, jealousy, greed, and so forth—in other words, motivation to be driven to murder.

8. There are no subplots in the mystery. The detective is never roman-tically involved with any of the characters (the way he may be in tough guy mysteries or police procedurals).

9. The classic detective is seldom (some would say never) in danger. He often provides the police with the information they need and they apprehend the criminal. Some detectives, like Nero Wolfe, never leave their homes and are so-called armchair detectives. They may bring the various suspects and the police to their homes for the final *dénouement* scene, but this does not always happen.

10. The explanation the classical detective gives of how he or she solved the murder must tie everything up in a logical manner; all of the clues must be explained and everything must make sense. The murderer must have had sufficient motivation and opportunity to kill the victim(s), the clues must all make sense (often having a meaning that readers missed), and readers must feel that the writer played fair with them, not introducing some *deus ex machina* or other factor that was extraneous to things. (There is no fantastic in who-dunits.) That is, when the detective explains how he or she solved the crime, the readers (or viewers) must recognize that they also could have solved the crime had they been perceptive enough and known enough to interpret the clues correctly. In some cases, stories explore subjects that readers find interesting. They involve arcane knowledge that readers lack, which is one reason they cannot solve the mystery.

11. There is one detective, one criminal, and one or more victims. The villain is not a professional criminal, is not the detective, and kills (or commits crimes) for personal reasons. Sometimes the person who is killed is a most unpleasant and nasty individual (who, in a sense, deserves to be killed) and readers feel some ambivalence about the killing because of this.

12. There are often conflicting stories by the witnesses (and people involved) about the details of the crime that have to be reconciled by the detective.

These rules give us a pretty good sense of the nature of the classic detective mystery, though as I mentioned above, there are numer-ous variations that are possible—and in some cases the rules are broken. Thus, in Agatha Christie's *Murder on the Orient Express* there are twelve murderers and in her *Who Killed Roger Akroyd* it is the detective who is the murderer. We see, then, that Christie wrote classic mysteries but also was quite an innovator.

I have not said anything about when mysteries take place; there is nothing to prevent a writer from creating a classic detective figure in ancient China or in the future. It is the nature of the detective and the crime that is committed, as well as the various rules that must be followed by the mystery writer that are crucial, not the era or time period when the crime was committed.

Psychoanalytic Perspectives on Classic Mysteries

Let me return to Freud's structural hypothesis, which argued that there are three agencies in the human psyche—the id (impulse), the ego (rationality), and the superego (conscience). In this typology I believe it is the detective who represents the ego function. The ego is connected with reason, with interpreting events in the world in order to maintain a balance between id and superego pressures. The murderer would be an id figure and the police, society, and so forth would be representatives of the superego—illustrated in Table 6.2.

In Freud's perspective, the id is the source of energy and is a necessary component of the psyche. It is when the id gets out of control and dominates the psyche that there is trouble. The superego element in the classic mystery (the police) lacks the power to control the id, or in this case find out who the murderer is, which is why the ego figure, the detective, is necessary. In a sense we can look upon mysteries as little morality fables in which we remind ourselves of the dangers and consequences of allowing our impulses free reign.

Martin Grotjahn (1966), a Freudian psychiatrist, has an interesting theory that explains our interest in murder mysteries. He points out that something like a quarter of all fiction published in the United States—and I would add that television and film as well—is dominated by crime and murder. Why might this be? His discussion of mystery stories in his book *Beyond Laughter: Humor and the Subconscious* offers some suggestions.

He starts by asserting that "we all harbor murderous wishes in our unconscious" and vaguely recognize this and feel guilty about

TABLE 6.2 Mystery Stories and the Psyche

Id	Ego	Superego (Perverted)
Murderer	Detective	Police, society
Kills	Discovers killer	Punishes
Lacks restraint	Reasons	Lacks intelligence

it (p. 154). The most important murder he is concerned about, let me suggest, is that of the parent of the opposite sex and is connected to the Oedipus complex. We are not aware of this feeling; it is buried deep down in our psyches. Thus we feel ambivalence when we read mysteries: one part of us (tied to repressed hostile tendencies) identifies with the murderer and the other generally identifies with the detective and, in some cases, with the murder victim. Suspense is generated by two things: the fear of being found out and the hope of getting away with the crime.

Our interest in mysteries is tied, Grotjahn (1966) suggests, to the interest we had when we were children in what went on in our parents bedrooms. He writes that

> Notwithstanding careful precautions taken by the parents, who do not wish to be the objects of their child's search for truth, almost every healthy child succeeds in making appropriate observation of the "primal scene." (p. 156)

Sometimes children observe dogs or other animals fornicating or hear stories from other children. Children, Grotjahn argues, see the primal scene as a fight in which the male triumphs and the female is conquered and hurt—and perhaps even killed. Grotjahn continues:

> The attempts to learn the facts of life is later symbolized in the search for the detailed facts of a crime, which lead to the discovery of the murderer. The interest in the mystery is a reactivation of the long-repressed interest in the bloody details of life and death, intercourse, menstruation, defloration, pregnancy, birth, delivery, and all the rest of it. The secret crime is the crime of the primal scene which a child is not supposed to witness. (p. 156)

The smart kid on the block, who knows all about sex, becomes the analogue to the detective, the mother (in disguise) is the victim, and the father is the murderer. In murder mysteries, suggests Grotjahn (1966), our curiosity is displaced from sex to crime, and the mystery story

> desexualizes our curiosity and idealizes it in the interest of justice. It is personified in the great detective who can investigate, combine, speculate, indulge in the infantile lust for uninhibited looking and listening without fear of reproach. (pp. 157, 158)

In this "game" we find the following: The detective is an outsider who works in unorthodox ways and is analogous to the curious child, investigating the primal scene; the police and authorities represent the parents, and want to keep the child in the dark. We know the real story of what went on in the bedroom when we are adults, Grotjahn adds, but we must continually rediscover it because in our unconscious we do not really believe it.

Thus we read mystery stories. On the conscious level we are looking for entertainment but on the unconscious level we are continually investigating the primal scene. When we were children we were all detectives and, as a result of our Oedipal complexes, we were all (potential) murderers.

Grotjahn's reading of mystery stories is a Freudian one and will, no doubt, strike many people as farfetched and perhaps even as ridiculous. And yet, how else can you explain the fascination these mysteries have for so many people and the dominance of crime and murder stories in the mass media? We read murder mysteries (or watch them on television and on film) to be entertained but why should this particular genre (and its various subgenres) entertain us and not other genres?

The Social Dimensions of Mysteries

Let us move from the psychological plane to the sociological one. What do these stories tell us about society and culture? There are so many mysteries from so many countries written in so many different styles that it is hard to make generalizations. But if we take the English variety of the classic mystery, we find in them, often, a reflection of the class differences that play such a large role in Engish society. I discussed some of the features of these texts earlier.

Many of these mysteries take place in a grand home or manor, there are servants, some of whom are of dubious morality, and there is a family or some kind of a grouping with various problematics and passions. There is a pleasure to be gained for the reader or viewer from being in such surroundings—a lifestyle which we cannot aspire to is ours (but only vicariously). There is often great affluence, there are beautiful women, handsome men, people with power and influence. And many of them, we also discover, are morally bankrupt and corrupt.

One thinks of Aristotle's notion that tragedy involves the fall of a "great man." A good classical murder mystery involves, in the same manner, the death of a person of some substance and importance: a business titan, a member of the royalty, for example. In the great homes, the butler does not do it (because one rule of the classic mystery is that a major character has to be the criminal) and the butler is not the primary victim of the killer. The butler may be killed after the main killing if, somehow, he learned something and found out who the killer is. But generally speaking, we do not find working-class elements being the major victims in classic crime stories.

We have a curiosity about how the rich and powerful live, a desire to snoop (voyeurism), and this is satisfied particularly well by the classic mystery story. That is because there is a murder which has to be investigated and the detective is required to dig deeply into everyone's doings, revealing, inevitably, all kinds of ugly things: sexual liaisons, dishonesty, skeletons in the closets (that is, ancient crimes) and, of course, murder. Thus we gain from this investigation both a satisfaction of our curiosity about how the upper classes live and, as a result of the various revelations, a sense of our moral superiority. We have the best of both worlds. We can, at times, participate, vicariously, in the killing of the victim (who often is a nasty person whose death is not a great loss to humanity) and the discovery of the murderer.

The classic mystery provides many gratifications to its readers and also, indirectly, reflects class differences, attitudes, belief structures and values, and other sociological phenomena found in the writer of the mystery and through the writer in the societies in which the stories are located.

In the next two chapters I will analyze two important texts: Dashiell Hammett's memorable tough guy mystery, *The Maltese Falcon*, and Agatha Christie's celebrated and innovative classical mystery, *Murder on the Orient Express*. Both of these novels are superbly written, with complex and interesting characters. And both have been made into excellent motion pictures.

Note

1. He wrote an important book on the fantastic: Todorov, T. (1973). *The Fantastic: A Structural Approach to a Literary Genre* and an interesting article on detective fiction, Todorov, T. (1988). "The typology of detective fiction."

PART II

Texts

The structuralist emphasis on the "constructedness" of human meaning represented a major advance. Meaning was neither a private experience nor a divinely ordained occurrence: it was the product of certain shared systems of signification. . . . Meaning was not "natural," a question of just looking and seeing, or something eternally settled; the way you interpreted your world was a function of the languages you had at your disposal, and there was evidently nothing immutable about these. Meaning was not something which all men and women intuitively shared, and then articulated in their various tongues and scripts: what meaning you were able to articulate depended on what script or speech you shared in the first place.

SOURCE: Eagleton, T. (1983, p. 107) *Literary Theory: An Introduction*. Minneapolis: University of Minnesota Press.

7

Murder on the Orient Express

Synopsis of the Story

Hercule Poirot, after being involved in a delicate case, is on his way back to England from Syria. He takes a train to Istanbul, where he hopes to spend a few days looking around, but when he checks into a hotel, the Tokatlian, he receives a telegram informing him that he must return to London immediately. While dining at the hotel, he meets, by chance, an old friend, M. Bouc, a director of Wagons Lit, who is also on his way back to Europe. Poirot discovers that, surprisingly, there is no room on the Simplon Orient (Express), which is departing that evening. But his friend Bouc, as an official of the line, tells him that he will get him a berth. One compartment, number sixteen, is always kept empty, Bouc tells Poirot. When they get to the train they discover that number sixteen is taken and all the berths have been reserved. However, one berth, in compartment seven, was reserved by an A. M. Harris, who has not arrived. Bouc arranges to have Poirot put in that berth, though Bouc later decides to move to a second class compartment and has Poirot moved to Bouc's compartment, number one. There is a curious assortment of people on the train. At lunch, with Bouc, Poirot "ran his eye thoughtfully" around the dining car and took stock of the thirteen people seated in it. Among the people he notices one man, a man of between sixty and seventy, who Poirot had noticed at the Tokatlian hotel, a man Poirot had decided was evil. When the dining car has emptied of everyone except Poirot and the man, he comes over to Poirot, asks if he is Hercule Poirot, introduces himself (Mr. Ratchett) and then asks Poirot to take a case. "My life has been threatened," Ratchett says. He offers Poirot twenty thousand dollars. Poirot refuses the job, saying he only takes cases that interest him. When Ratchett asks why, Poirot answers, "If you will forgive me for being personal—I do not like your face M. Ratchett."

That evening Ratchett is killed—stabbed a dozen times. The next morning, when Poirot awakens, he discovers two things: the train has been snowed in and has halted near some city in Yugoslavia and that Ratchett has been murdered. Bouc asks Poirot to take the case and solve it before the Yugoslavian police get involved. Poirot agrees.

He questions all of the passengers. One of them, a Mrs. Hubbard, says a strange man had been in her compartment, a man who disappeared in the middle of the night. Poirot eventually discovers the identity of Ratchett—he really was Canetti, a powerful and very wealthy gang leader. He had kidnapped and murdered a little child, Daisy Armstrong, many years before. As a result of this crime, Daisy's mother gave birth prematurely to a dead child, the mother died of grief, the father shot himself, and a nursemaid (who was under suspicion) committed suicide. Canetti, as a result of a legal technicality, was not convicted. He then disappeared, took an assumed name, and spent a number of years traveling.

Poirot is able to figure out that everyone on the train was connected with the Armstrongs, one way or another, and that everyone took part in a ritual murder of Canetti/Ratchett. On the other hand, there was the man who supposedly had hidden in a compartment (and Poirot had actually seen someone who could have been this man) who could be the murderer. Poirot offers two explanations: one involving the people on the train and the other putting the blame on the mysterious man. It is decided that the second explanation will be offered to the Yugoslavian police when they arrive.

The Classical Detective Novel

We have already discussed the attributes of the classical detective novel. *Murder on the Orient Express* is a wonderful example of this, except that it has one remarkable innovation. Usually there is but one murderer; in this novel there are twelve. Everyone on the train was involved in the murder and all were "linked."

Christie continually gives us hints to this effect, but because we expect only one murderer, we take no notice. For example, when Bouc is having lunch with Poirot and he surveys the people in the dining car, we find the following dialogue:

> "If I had but the pen of Balzac! I would depict this scene . . ."
> "It is an idea, that," said Poirot.
> "Ah, you agree? It has not been done, I think? And yet—it lends itself to romance, my friend. All around us are people, of all classes, of all nationalities, of all ages. For three days these people, these strangers to one another, are brought together. They sleep and eat under one roof, they cannot get away from each other. At the end of three days they part, they go their several ways, never perhaps to see each other again."
> "And yet," said Poirot, "suppose an accident——
> "Ah, no, my friend—"
> "From your point of view it would be regrettable, I agree. But nevertheless let us just for one moment suppose it. Then, perhaps, all these here are linked together—by death." (Christie, 1940, p. 29, 30)

That evening Poirot does not sleep well. He hears a cry at 12.37 A.M. from Ratchett's compartment, which adjoins his. But Ratchett then responds, in French, to the porter that nothing has happened. Then he hears the water running in Ratchett's compartment, shuffling footsteps, and so forth as he dozes off. A bit later Poirot is wakened by someone bumping into his door. When Poirot opens it he sees "a woman, wrapped in a scarlet kimono . . . retreating from him."

And finally, when he wakes up next morning, he discovers everyone in the dining car moaning about the train being stuck in the snow. Christie writes: "Any barriers there might have been between the passengers had now quite broken down. All were united by a common misfortune." We do not, of course, recognize the significance of this passage. Only after we have finished the novel do we see that Christie has given us yet another clue.

There are a number of others as well.

Just after Ratchett's body has been discovered, Poirot interviews Ratchett's secretary MacQueen.

Bouc finds MacQueen's answers to be convincing and suggests that at least one person on the train seems to be innocent.

"Me, I suspect everybody till the last minute," is Poirot's interesting reply. The significance of the term *everybody* is lost on us as we read the book, until the end when we discover that everybody was involved in the killing.

Near the end of the book, when Poirot has discovered that Ratchett is Canetti and that some people on the train were connected to the Armstrong household, Bouc says something important:

> "Nothing would surprise me now," said M. Bouc. "Nothing! Even if everybody in the train proved to have been in the Armstrong household, I should not express surprise."
>
> "That is a very profound remark," said Poirot.

Bouc is telegraphing the surprising conclusion to the story, but readers still do not appreciate the significance of this remark.

The bulk of the novel involves Poirot using his famous "little grey cells of the mind" to discover who the people on the train are, how they are linked together, and how they killed Ratchett.

It is interesting to compare this novel and Hercule Poirot with *The Maltese Falcon* and Sam Spade. We find there are a considerable number of differences between the two works (Table 7.1).

I may be exaggerating slightly, but I think you can see that these two genres are quite different. All murder mysteries involve deception, but in *The Maltese Falcon*, Sam Spade is as deceptive as everyone else. Everyone lies, constantly, to everyone else—and nobody can be trusted. In *Murder on the Orient Express*, the deceptions are all aimed at Poirot, whose task it is to cut through the false clues and fake alibis and discover who killed Ratchett.

TABLE 7.1 Comparison of the Two Novels

Murder on the Orient Express	*The Maltese Falcon*
Hercule (mythic figure)	Sam (common name)
Poirot (pearlike man)	Spade (digger)
Ridiculous looking man	Rugged, handsome man
All mind	Action (plus brains)
Sentimental	Unsentimental
Revenge the motive	Greed basic factor
Moral ambiguity	Code of ethics
Aristocracy, other classes	Seedy elements
Ritual murder	Unplanned murders
Obvious villain	Secret villainess
Humanist detective	Cynical detective
International locale	San Francisco locale
Deception of Poirot basic	Everyone deceives

Literary Style

Hammett has been lauded for the wonderful dialogue in *The Maltese Falcon*, but Christie also has a marvelous ear for description and dialogue. Her writing is extremely simple and almost transparent. Her description of the Russian princess, Natalia Dragomiroff, is typical.

Her small toad-like face looked even yellower than the day before. She was certainly ugly, and yet, like the toad, she had eyes like jewels, dark and imperious, revealing latent energy and an intellectual force that could be felt at once. (1940, p. 114)

Christie believes that the eyes are the mirror of the soul, that seems evident. Her description of Ratchett also focused on his eyes.

His slightly bald head, his domed forehead, the smiling mouth that displayed a very white set of false teeth—all seemed to speak of a benevolent personality. Only the eyes belied this assumption. They were small, deep-set and crafty. As the man, making some remark to his young companion, glanced across the room, his gaze stopped on Poirot for a moment and just for that second there was a strange malevolence, an unnatural intensity in the glance. (1940, p. 23)

When he walks by Poirot in the hotel, Poirot has a distinct feeling that a wild animal, something savage, has passed by him.

Poirot, on the other hand, is described as "a little man with enormous moustaches," a man with "an egg shaped head," "a ridiculous looking little man. The sort of man one could never take seriously." It is his mind that fascinates us and his various personality traits. A major part of the book involves Poirot interviewing the people on the train and getting evidence from them. The dialogues in these interviews are very matter of fact and simple. It is the various slips that the people on the train (all of whom are suspects) make when chatting with Poirot that add up to a kind of gestalt and enable him to solve the crime. That and his wide-ranging knowledge, which helps him see through various misleading clues that have been left for him, to throw him off the track.

When Christie writes dialogue, she tends to avoid terms like *said* and *responded* and *asked*. We have people speaking to one another, as the following passage in which the valet is interviewed demonstrates.

> "Your compartment was—"
> "The end second-class one, sir. Next to the dining car."
> "That is No. 4?"
> "Yes, sir."
> "Is there anyone in with you?"
> "Yes, sir. A big Italian fellow."
> "Does he speak English?"
> "Well, a kind of English, sir." The valet's tone was deprecating.
> "He's been in America—Chicago, I understand." (1940, p. 93)

This dialogue is very similar to that found in plays and part of Christie's appeal, I believe, is due to what we might call her theatrical style of writing dialogue. In that this is a detective novel, readers will be carefully scrutinizing this dialogue, simple as it seems to be, for clues—as they match wits with Hercule Poirot and try to discover who the murderer is before Poirot reveals it to everyone.

TABLE 7.2 Polar Oppositions in *Murder on the Orient Express*

Ratchett	People on the Train
Evil (a rat)	Good
Looks evil	Look different
Tries to hire Poirot	Try to mislead Poirot
Has killed Daisy Armstrong	Have suffered from Daisy's death
Has escaped punishment	Punish Ratchett for crimes
Is killed	Kill Ratchett

Polar Oppositions in
Murder on the Orient Express

Let me suggest that the following oppositions (Table 7.2) are found in the story. These oppositions reveal the hidden or latent meaning of the text according to Lévi-Strauss (1967).

Poirot mediates between these two characters (we must think of the twelve passengers as functioning as one collective "character" here) and ultimately comes to a decision about what should be done as far as revealing who the murderer is. He poses a solution in such a way that his colleagues, Bouc and a Dr. Constantine, who was on an adjoining coach and is involved in determining when Ratchett was killed and what the different stab wounds mean, can pin the murder on a fictitious mysterious stranger.

The novel is, we see, really about crime and punishment and the question of whether extralegal methods can rightfully be used to punish criminals who have, due to legal technicalities, escaped punishment. In the case of Ratchett/Casetti, we are not only told about his horrendous crime and the disastrous consequences of this crime (which affected all of the passengers on the train) but it is also suggested that he has kidnapped and murdered other children.

In Chapter 8, "The Armstrong Kidnapping Case," there is an important bit of dialogue. After hearing about Casetti we find the following lines spoken by Bouc and Poirot:

"Ah! quel animal!" Mr. Bouc's tone was redolent of heart-felt disgust. "I cannot regret that he is dead—not at all!"
"I agree with you."

So Poirot and his friend Bouc have already agreed, in a sense, that Casetti's death is no great loss. Thus when a self-appointed jury of twelve people condemned Ratchett to death and acted as his executioner, there is good reason to anticipate that Bouc will opt for the explanation that will allow the passengers to go free. He chooses to accept the notion that "a small dark man with a womanish voice" who had been in Mrs. Hubbard's compartment was the killer.

At the *dénouement*, when Poirot explains how he figured out that a dozen people on the train (one passenger, a countess, did not stab Ratchett) killed Ratchett, Mrs. Hubbard, who was in reality Linda Arden, Daisy Armstrong's grandmother and a famous actress, offers a poignant statement.

"Well," she said, "you know everything now, M. Poirot. What are you going to do about it? . . . It wasn't only that he was responsible for my daughter's death and her child's and that of the other child who might have been alive and happy now. It was more then that: there had been other children kidnapped before Daisy, and there might be others in the future. Society had condemned him—we were only carrying out the sentence." (1940, p. 255)

Ethical Dilemmas

The book presents us with several ethical dilemmas, for which there are no simple answers. Casetti is portrayed as a monster and was described by M. Bouc as "an animal." Poirot agrees that his death is no loss to humanity. And he is portrayed as not only monstrously evil, but still dangerous, still a threat.

Is it right to violate the law to uphold it? And is it right to allow a person who is dangerous and who has killed children and destroyed the lives of many people to go free because of legal technicalities? Where does justice lie in this situation? And what does one do about people who have suffered from the acts of an evil person, who are victims, and who have transgressed in a good cause?

Poirot is quite different from Sam Spade. He is like a dog who has caught a bird and will not let go. Poirot, on the other hand, is somewhat more philosophical about life and human frailty. He is a man of intellect who recognizes the problematical nature of human existence, who understands that we must often live in a world of ambiguity, that conflict is part of life and so is evil.

Social and Political Significance of *Murder on the Orient Express*

Ultimately, in this novel and in the classical detective novel in general, we find the power of mind triumphant. Often the police, the bureaucratic entity in society that deals with crime, need help and that is where the classical detective, who is not a member of the police force, comes in.

This novel is essentially about elites. Poirot had been summoned to Syria by a general and had performed various services for him. He meets a friend, M. Bouc, who is a director of the Wagon-Lits railroad company. Daisy Armstrong, the little girl who was kidnapped, was from a wealthy family. Her grandmother, Linda Arden, was "the most famous tragic American actress of her day." And her father was from a very wealthy family on the American side and an aristocratic family on the English side. There are people from other social strata in the story, who were profoundly affected by the kidnapping and killing, but the novel really revolves around elite and elevated elements of society.

The message of *Murder on the Orient Express* is that social harmony must be maintained by cooperation among all elements (elites, common people) in pursuit of their common good. Casetti is a deviant, a criminal individualist who has no concern with laws or the mores of society, and as such, must be punished. If that society, because of legal technicalities, cannot punish him, others (who were victimized by him) must take on that extralegal responsibility. This is because justice must be done (when the law turns blind) and victims of criminals have a right of retribution. Actually, it was not that justice turned blind but that Casetti was able to use his money to get off in the case. This we find out at the end of the story.

By chance it turns out the most immediate victims of Casetti were Jewish. Daisy Armstrong's mother's family name was Goldenberg and because descent among Jews is matrilineal, Daisy Armstrong was Jewish. Thus Casetti was responsible for the death of three Jews: Daisy, her mother, and the child her mother was carrying. Ironically, the one member of the party who does not stab Casetti is Daisy Armstrong's aunt, Helena Andrenyi, who had married a Hungarian count. Her husband stabbed Casetti in her place.

This matter is important in the story, in that it helps Poirot figure out what is going on, but it is not of major significance otherwise. What is crucial is that a sadistic criminal has destroyed a family from the elite social strata (as well as ruining the lives of those connected with them) and must be punished. In a conversation between Princess Dragomiroff, Bouc, and Poirot we find the following exchange.

> "I believe, Messieurs, in loyalty—to one's friends and one's family and one's caste."
> "You do not believe in doing your utmost to further the ends of justice?"
> "In this case I consider that justice—strict justice—has been done."
> (1940, p. 222)

That is the voice of a member of what Wildavsky (1986) would call "hierarchical elites" talking—about loyalty, family and caste, very traditional values. At times, so the novel suggests, the elites who run society must keep secrets from people, must use deception for the general good. That is the case in *Murder on the Orient Express*, in which all of the suspects lie continually—but for a good purpose. They are forced to lie because justice has, in this particular case, been blind and let a monstrous criminal go free.

This novel and classical detective novels in general can be seen as metaphors showing the role of the intelligentsia in society. Poirot looks ridiculous and is the kind of "little" man one cannot take seriously, we are told. But he has a powerful intellect that modern society needs. In an information society, it is people with intellectual power who are crucial. But also, the novel shows, empathetic understanding or what we would call, in America, big hearts.

"It is all a matter of the intellect," Poirot says at one point, but as the conclusion of the novel shows, there is more to it than that.

We have shown how, in different ways, the mystery story is involved with the problem of evil; how it provides us with a hero who answers deep-seated needs. . . . It is time to anatomize the underlying metaphysical pattern—*the detective story is modern man's Passion Play.*

In the beginning is the murder, and the world is sorely out of joint. There appears the detective-hero and his foil, the latter representing the blindness of ordinary mortals—Dr. Watson, or the police, or, if the hero is a policeman, his bumbling associates. The detective is a man like the rest of us, with his share of human failings—Nero Wolfe swills beer; Maigret is helpless without his pipe; Hammer goes in for venery. But this mortal has the Call—he is a Savior. In him is Grace, and we know that he will bring light. . . .

By his personality, his deeds, his methods, the hero bears witness to a system of belief, a secular credo for a religious doctrine. He is the apostle of science, like Holmes, or of Pure Reason, like Hercule Poirot. . . . Whatever system of belief the hero acts out will, for the duration, infuse something of itself into the reader. He will find himself saving the world with a borrowed credo which is temporarily *his.* And herein lies the hidden seduction of the whodunit. Mystery stories are blood-stained fairy tales which enact the cycle, Paradise Lost—Paradise Sought For—Paradise Regained. *They allow us to play, vicariously, the role of different kinds of Savior.*

SOURCE: Roloe, C. J. (1957). Simenon and Spillane: The Metaphysics of Murder for the Millions. In Bernard Rosenberg and David Manning White (Eds.), *Mass Culture: The Popular Arts in America* (pp. 174, 175). Free Press.

8

The Maltese Falcon:
The Hard-Boiled Detective Novel

The Maltese Falcon is a murder mystery but it is more than that. It has a remarkable cast of characters, deals with issues of considerable significance (as far as ethics, the destructive nature of greed, and relations between men and women are concerned) and was made into a memorable movie.

The Maltese Falcon:
A Brief Synopsis

The story, which takes place in San Francisco, begins with a visit by a woman calling herself Miss Wonderly (she later reveals her true name as Brigid O'Shaugnessy) to Sam Spade's office. He has a detective agency with Miles Archer. She is described by Spade's secretary, Effie Perine, as a "knockout." She tells him her sister has been spirited away by one Floyd Thursby and she wants to find her and bring her back home before their parents return from a trip to Europe. In the middle of the interview, Miles Archer comes in and volunteers to shadow her and Thursby that evening. That evening Archer is shot and killed, at very close range, in an alley near the Stockton street tunnel. Later, Thursby's body is found; he was also shot.

Spade is visited later by Joel Cairo, a duplicitous Levantine who wants to hire him to find a statuette of a black bird and says he will pay him five-thousand dollars to do so. When Effie goes home, Cairo pulls a gun on Spade. Spade elbows Cairo and knocks him out, and then goes over the contents of his pockets. He later comes in contact with Wilmer Cook, a "kid," a young hood (who is, we later find out, romantically involved with Cairo) and finally with Casper Gutman, a very fat man who has been pursuing the bird, a Maltese Falcon, for seventeen years, all over the world, because he believes it is made of gold and jewels and is worth a fortune.

Gutman sent Brigid to Constantinople, where she joined up with Cairo to get the bird. She decided to double-cross Gutman. She had Cairo put in jail for a while and went to Hong Kong with Thursby. There she gave the bird to one Captain Jacobi, master of a boat called *La Paloma*. He and Brigid get together but are interrupted by Gutman and his crew. Jacobi escapes, after being shot by Wilmer, and brings the bird to Spade. Spade puts it in a terminal. Eventually he gets together with Gutman and his crew and convinces Gutman to use Wilmer as a "fall guy." Otherwise, Spade says he will not give Gutman the bird. Gutman agrees and Spade gets him the bird.

When Gutman unwraps the Maltese Falcon he discovers that it is made of lead. He decides that he got the wrong falcon in Constantinople and decides to return there immediately. When he leave, Spade calls the police and tells them to pick up Gutman and, also, that he has the gun used to kill Archer. Then he confronts Brigid and informs her that he knows who killed Miles—she did. And that he is turning her in to the police. She tries to use her feminine wiles to dissuade him, but does not succeed. He explains that he has a code of ethics and that he does not want to be taken for a sucker by Brigid, the way everyone else has been.

This summary offers a broad outline of the plot and functions as a background or overview that helps make sense of some of the topics to be discussed.

The Hard-Boiled Detective

Dashiell Hammett's *The Maltese Falcon* is generally considered to be one of the outstanding hard-boiled (or tough guy) detective novels. Its hero, Sam Spade, is worldly, cynical, and decidedly unsentimental. He is described by Hammett as a "blond Satan" with a jutting chin and broad shoulders, a rugged six-footer who knows the score. It is mostly in the dialogue that Spade's toughness is revealed, though Spade also can be quite violent at times.

For example, after Spade's partner, Miles Archer, has been killed, Spade is visited at his apartment by a detective, Tom Polhaus, and his boss, Lieutenant Dundy. They want to know whether Miles was working on a case and if so, who their client was. Spade will not tell them. He says he has to talk to his client first.

> "You'll tell it to me or you'll tell it in court," Dundy said hotly. "This is murder and don't you forget it."
> "Maybe. And here's something for you not to forget, sweetheart. I'll tell it or not as I damned please. It's a long while since I burst out crying because policemen didn't like me." (1972, p. 20)

This confrontation establishes Spade's independence and toughness and also sets up one of the main elements in the plot—the suspicion the police have that Spade killed Archer because Spade was known to have been involved with Archer's wife, Iva.

Brigid O'Shaughnessy's Line

There is a wonderful scene involving Brigid and Sam that takes place at her apartment. She reveals her real name, then we read the following:

> "Mr. Spade, tell me the truth." Her voice quivered on the verge of hysteria. Her face had become haggard around desperate eyes. "Am I to blame for—for last night." (1972, p. 34)

Spade shook his head. "Not unless there are things I don't know about," he said. (1972, p. 34)

A short while later she asks him whether he thinks she had anything to do with the murders. He asks her whether she did and she says "no."

Then he asks what he should tell the police and what is going on. She says she cannot tell him and then gives him her "line."

> "I haven't lived a good life," she cried. "I've been bad—worse than you could know—but I'm not all bad. Look at me, Mr Spade. You know I'm not all bad don't you? You can see that, can't you? Then can't you trust me a little? Oh, I'm so alone and afraid, and I've got nobody to help me if you won't help me." (1972, pp. 35, 36)

She continues in this way for quite awhile. Spade's answer is interesting:

> "You won't need much of anybody's help. You're good. You're very good. It's chiefly your eyes, I think, and that throb you get into your voice when you say things like 'Be generous, Mr. Spade.'" (1972, p. 30)

He is a tough guy who recognizes Brigid's playacting for what it is. What she does not know, and what readers do not know at this moment, is that Spade is pretty sure that Brigid has killed Miles Archer. Thus, he is, in a sense, toying with her—playing along with her until he sees how things can be resolved and he can prove that she actually killed Miles. He knows that she is a liar and eventually even gets her to admit it. "I am a liar," she admits. "I have always been a liar" (1972, p. 92).

At the *dénouement*, when Sam tells Brigid that he is turning her over to the police, she suddenly recognizes something.

> "But—but, Sam, you can't. Not after what we've been to each other. You can't—"
> "Like hell I can't."

She took a long trembling breath. "You've been playing with me? Only pretending you cared—to trap me? You didn't care at all? You didn't—don't—I-love me?"

"I think I do," Spade said. "What of it?" (1972, pp. 223, 224)

In fact, Brigid is correct. But, as Sam points out, she had set Sam up and had knocked off Miles "in cold blood, just like swatting a fly." Sam adds that she has double-crossed everyone and that he will not play the sap for her, that he has got to hand her over to the police, otherwise he is sunk. In other words, she cannot use her sexuality to manipulate him the way she has manipulated the others. Besides, he explains, he has a code of ethics that he follows and even though Miles was a "louse," Sam still had to follow his code.

Sam Spade's Code of Ethics

This code appears at the very end of the story, just a few pages before the novel concludes. He has just told Brigid that she did not do him any harm by killing Miles, because he was a louse. She wonders why he is going to turn her over. He explains:

Listen. When a man's partner is killed he's supposed to do something about it. It doesn't make any difference what you thought of him. He was your partner and you're supposed to do something about it. Then it happens we were in the detective business. Well, when one of your organization gets killed it's bad business to let the killer get away with it. It's bad all around—bad for that one organization, bad for every detective everywhere. Third, I'm a detective and expecting me to run criminals down and then let them go free is like asking a dog to catch a rabbit and let it go. It can be done, all right, and sometimes it is done, but it's not the natural thing. . . . Fourth, no matter what I wanted to do now it would be absolutely impossible for me to let you go without having myself dragged to the gallows with the others. Next, I've no reason in God's world to think I can trust you and if I did this and got away with it you'd have something on me that you could use whenever you happened to want to. That's five of them. The sixth would be that, since I've also got something on you, I couldn't be sure you

wouldn't decide to shoot a hole in *me* someday. Seventh, I don't even
like the idea of thinking that there might be one chance in a hundred
that you'd played me for a sucker. . . . Now on the other side we've
got what? All we've got is the fact that maybe you love me and maybe
I love you. (1972, pp. 226, 227)

When Brigid exclaims that she knows how he feels he replies that
she does not, and that she cannot count on her sexuality to control
him the way she has counted on it in the past.

So he turns her over to the police. The novel comes to an end
with Effie mentioning that she'd read all about the case in the
morning paper and expressing incredulity. "You did that, Sam, to
her?" There is a kind of duality reflected here—a set of oppostions
between the logic and rationality of men and the emotionality and
intuitiveness of women.

"What do you think of Wonderly?" Sam had asked Effie early in
the novel. "I'm for her," Effie had replied, "without hesitation."
"She's got too many names," Spade mused. "I don't care if she's
got all the names in the phone book. That girl is all right, and you
know it," answered Effie. "I wonder," he replied (1972, p. 43).

The Characters

We have, then, quite a collection of characters. Brigid O'Shaugnessy
is a double-dealing compulsive liar who uses her looks to control
men and kills Miles "in cold blood, just like swatting a fly." Casper
Gutman is a grotesque fat man who spends seventeen years in a
futile search for the Maltese Falcon, an ironic reversal of the quest
theme (it is usually heroes who are sent on quests, to rescue
maidens, etc.). His greed and passion to obtain the bird is so great
that he is willing to sacrifice Wilmer Cook as a fall-guy, even though
Gutman explains "I feel towards Wilmer just exactly as if he were
my own son." Joel Cairo is an effeminate homosexual, who works
for Gutman but whose loyalty is questionable. Wilmer Cook, the
"kid," is a psychopathic killer who is also a homosexual and has,
it is suggested, a relationship with Cairo. Cook turns, finally, on his

TABLE 8.1 Polar Oppositions in the Text

Brigid/Associates	Gutman/Associates
Sex	Money
BRIGID (frigid?)	GUTMAN (all gut)
Floyd Thursby	Joel Cairo
Miles Archer	Wilmer Cook
"Donor" Figure	Quest Figure
Innocence (pseudo)	Criminality (bumbling)
Beautiful	Ugly
Tragic	Pathetic

"father" figure, Gutman, and kills him, in revenge. And caught in the middle of all this is Sam Spade.

Let me offer a paradigmatic analysis of this text in Table 8.1. It offers the basic polar opposition that is found in the book and reveals the meaning of the story. We find Brigid and those associated with her on one side, Gutman and his associates on the other side, and Sam Spade (and various police figures with whom he has an ambiguous relationship) in the middle, mediating between the two polarities.

Sam Spade, like all mythic heroes (so Lévi-Strauss, the French structural anthropologist suggests) mediates between opposing forces and reconciles them, one way or another. He is able to resist Brigid's duplicity and sexual power, unlike Thursby and Archer, who were victims of it, and Gutman's duplicity, his use of money and (in the person of the kid) of violence. It is his code of ethics and his recognition that Brigid has played everyone for a sucker that enables him to resist her, even though, as he puts it, he "may" love her. "Don't be too sure I'm as crooked as I'm supposed to be," he tells her (1972, p. 227).

Earlier it was suggested that in mysteries there are two victims: the first one is the victim of the killer and the second one is the killer, who becomes the victim of the detective. In *The Maltese Falcon* we find that sexuality used to manipulate and control people is as destructive as greed. Both Brigid and Gutman become carried away with their passions and ultimately destroy themselves. They are both *id* figures: Brigid (sexuality) and Gutman (food, money) who show how dangerous it is when desires overcome any sense of morality in people. Spade, of course, is also duplicitous and not presented as the most moral person in the world (he does have a relationship with Miles Archer's wife and he does lead Brigid along, to some degree) but he is dealing with people who are quite evil and has to defend himself as best he can.

Social Types in *The Maltese Falcon*

We have a variety of social types in the book, which are illustrated in Table 8.2.

We have dealt with most of the people mentioned above, with the exception of Charles Flitcraft. The story of Flitcraft represents a remarkable innovation in the detective novel, for the Flitcraft episode has, on the face of it, nothing to do with the story. It is a story within a story, and offers an early example of what might be described as existential epiphany. While Spade and Brigid are waiting for Cairo to visit them, Spade tells Brigid about Flitcraft. Flitcraft went off to work one day, went to lunch, and mysteriously, with only fifty or sixty dollars in his pocket, disappeared. "He went like that," Spade said, "like a fist when you open your hand."

Flitcraft was the quintessential common man—he was married, had two children, a house in the suburbs of Tacoma, a new car, a good job—and seemed to settle into a classic middle-class lifestyle. One day, while going to lunch, he walked by an office building that was being erected and a beam fell near him. He had had a brush with death, though all that happened was that a piece of concrete chipped off and hit him in the cheek. This experience changed him. "He felt," Spade says, "like somebody had taken the lid off life and let him look at the works."

Spade continues:

Flitcraft had been a good citizen and a good husband and father, not by any outer compulsion, but simply because he was a man who was most comfortable in step with his surroundings. He had been raised

TABLE 8.2 Social Types in the Text

Character	Social Type
Casper Gutman	Wealthy classes
Joel Cairo	Deviance, foreign cultures
Wilmer Cook	Psychotic killer
Charles Flitcraft	The common man
Brigid O'Shaugnessy	Femme fatale
Sam Spade	Cynical, skeptical, marginal occupation
Tom Polhaus	Governmental bureaucracy

that way. The people he knew were like that. The life he knew was a clean orderly sane responsible affair. Now a falling beam had shown him that life was fundamentally none of these things. He, the good citizen-husband-father could be wiped out between office and restaurant by the accident of a falling beam. He knew then that men died as haphazard like that, and lived only while blind chance spared them. (Hammett, 1972, p. 66)

Flitcraft did not return home that evening. He turned his back on his whole life; he went to Seattle, then to San Francisco, and eventually to Spokane, where he took an assumed name, Charles Pierce, married a woman, had a baby son, and was living as conventional a life as he had led before. Spade at the time was working for a large detective agency in Seattle when Mrs. Flitcraft came in and said that a man resembling her husband had been seen in Tacoma. Spade went to investigate the situation and discovered that the man, Charles Pierce, was Flitcraft. Flitcraft explained to Spade what had happened to him with the beam. Spade understood Flitcraft's story but Mrs. Flitcraft could not. The Flitcrafts got a divorce on the quiet and everything "was swell," as Spade put it.

"How perfectly fascinating," replies Brigid, who dismisses the story and returns to her theme of being utterly dependent on Spade. She has no interest in the story and, like Flitcraft's wife, cannot understand the significance of what happened to him when he was almost killed by the beam. Spade can understand because he is just the opposite of a person like Flitcraft.

Spade lives a life in which he is in constant danger, in which he is thrown into contact with all kinds of menacing and duplicitous people, has often faced death and has "adjusted" to it. Spade is cynical. He believes that people's actions are motivated mainly by self-interest and that he must exercise self-control and independence to survive. And he is skeptical. He knows from experience that people often lie, so it is best to take everything people tell you with a grain of salt. As such he is prepared to deal with the people he finds himself involved with. Nothing really surprises him. Brigid, on the other hand, is unprepared for surprises. Although she is a liar and someone who double-crosses people without a second thought, she is amazed when Spade refuses to let his feelings for her dominate his behavior.

"You've been playing with me? Only pretending you cared—to trap me? You didn't care at all? You didn't—don't—I-love me?" To which Spade replied "I think I do. . . . What of it?" In many respects, I would argue, Spade's cynicism and skepticism are reflections of typical American personality traits. We have a society that stresses the "self-made man and woman" and that leads to cynicism and skepticism. You are, on your own, responsible for your future and due to the fact that everyone is pursuing his or her own self-interest, you can only trust yourself in the final analysis. There is even an element of stoicism in Sam Spade that also is, I believe, reflected in American character—the freedom from passion and emotion and the acceptance of the fact that "beams" fall on people from time to time (that is, accidents of fate happen) and we must recognize this and live with this knowledge.

Adding to this is the notion that government and bureaucracies are a problem and more of a nuisance than a help. Tom Polhaus and Lt. Dundy, representatives of the political order, are misguided and think that Spade killed Archer or Thursby—or both. The tough guy detective has to solve the crime to avoid being suspected or convicted by the dumb cops. In the same way, the individual must prove himself or herself by being a success in the world; otherwise, there is doubt that cannot be allayed.

In these respects, then, Sam Spade is a paradigmatic hero, who reflects basic American personality traits and philosophical beliefs.

That may be why so many Americans find him so resonant a figure. He is the classic individualist, fighting against a blind and stupid police bureaucracy (representing what Wildavsky would call hierarchical elites) and a vicious and perverse group of criminals. Gutman and his associates show the danger of entrepreneurship that is out of control. Gutman is grotesque, morally as well as physically, who has squandered seventeen years of his life in pursuit of wealth, as represented by the Maltese Falcon. Brigid O'Shaugnessy is also an individualist, but she is one who lies continually, has no sense of loyalty to anyone, has used her physical beauty to manipulate men, and kills without a second thought.

Spade on the other hand, shows the virtue of a principled individualism for as his speech to Brigid about the rules motivating his behavior shows, he has what political scientists call *a theory of obligation.* He may be cynical and skeptical and stoical, but he also has a sense of duty and loyalty. *The Maltese Falcon* is a classic hard-boiled mystery story, but it is also a morality tale—a fable that reveals the danger society faces from people without principles, without a sense of social responsibility. Sam Spade may not be an angel, but he is, in his own way, a good citizen.

It is argued that the high literature of post-Modernism is characterized by its self-conscious fictionality, and lack of character and plot. But, if these critics paid more attention to current popular culture, they would see that most of their presuppositions about literacy, narrative, genre, openness and closure, the status of the fictive, the activity of the reader (read "reader-player," "reader-coder," "reader-programmer") are challenged by the everyday activities and resourcefulness of the kids playing fiction-games. Most of the fiction dealt with by young males outside of what they view on TV are those beheld or enacted in sports events constructed on fictional legal codes and in TV and computer games in which audience members themselves take part in enacting protagonist parts and making decisions in a narrative development— simultaneously playing the part of protagonist, author, and critic. This is the kind of high-level critical activity that makes reader community studies seem pallid—not with lack of theory, but with lack of wide empirical input to theory building. (We go back to Resnais's *Last Year at Marienbad* and the influence upon Resnais of *Mandrake the Magician!*)

SOURCE: Denney, R. (1989). *The Astonished Muse.* New Brunswick, NJ: Transaction Publishers.

9

Dr. No

A Popular Hero

I have already dealt with *Dr. No* in some detail—I offered a synopsis of the story as well as both a syntagmatic (Proppian) and paradigmatic (Lévi-Straussian) analysis of the text. I have chosen to deal with James Bond because he is, according to Tony Bennett and Janet Woollacott (1987), more than just the principal character in a series of books and films. He is, instead, a popular hero of enormous cultural, social, and political significance. In fact, they argue that "Bond is somewhat more than 'literature's most popular spy,' however. He is arguably the most popular—in the sense of widely known—figure of the post-war period, if not of this century" (p. 11). The first Bond novel, *Casino Royale*, appeared in paperback in 1955, so he has been around for almost forty years. *Dr. No* was the sixth Bond adventure, published in its paperback version in 1960.

Bennett and Woollacott provide statistics that show that something like 30 million Bond novels have been sold in paperback in Great Britain. To this we must add the Bond novels sold in America and the various Bond films, which sparked interest in the books. We end up with a figure of enormous impact and resonance, with worldwide appeal. There is good reason, then, to deal with a James

Bond story as a representative of the spy genre, even though there are other subgenres in spy literature—"civil servant" spies who work in large bureaucratic organizations and spend their time finding moles, spies who come in from the cold—and other kinds of spy stories as well. Not all spies are superheroes like Bond who have exciting adventures and spend a good deal of time in various exotic locales making love to beautiful women in the course of their duties.

Bond is, in certain respects, much closer to the tough guy American private eye, but true to the spy genre Bond is involved with matters of worldwide significance (saving the free world from various madmen). He travels to many exotic locales (the world is his oyster, not some city), he is a member of a governmental organization involved with espionage and his mission is not to find murderers but to prevent villains from gaining power and world domination.

I chose *Dr. No* because I think it is one of the more interesting Bond adventures and it also was the first Bond film, appearing in 1962. In addition, it has received a considerable amount of attention from critics.

Umberto Eco on *Dr. No*

Bennett and Woollacott discuss a Proppian analysis that Umberto Eco has made of *Dr. No* that differs somewhat from the one I offered earlier. Eco argues there are "nine moves" in all Bond stories, though they do not always have the same sequence. The plots of the Bond novels, then, are structurally similar. And, in addition, they are essentially variations of the traditional fairy tale, which is an archetype for them (and, as I have argued, other narrative genres).

These actions (similar to what Propp [1968] called *functions*), the typical features of the Bond plot, are:

1. M. gives Bond a task
2. The villain appears to Bond (sometimes in a vicarious form)

TABLE 9.1 Polar Opposition in Typical Bond Plot

Bond	The Villain
Free world	Soviet Union
Great Britain	Non-Anglo Saxon countries
Ideals	Power
Duty	Ideology
Chance	Planning
Luxury	Discomfort
Moderation	Excess
Innocence	Perversion
Loyalty	Disloyalty

3. Bond gives a "check" to the villain or the villain to Bond
4. "The girl" appears.
5. Bond possesses the girl or starts the process of seduction
6. The villain captures Bond and, either simultaneously or before or after, the girl.
7. The villain tortures Bond and, in some cases, the girl.
8. Bond vanquishes the villain, killing him and his representatives (or helps in their killing)
9. Bond makes love to the girl but he loses her: she leaves him or is killed.

These nine actions can be applied to *Dr. No* quite easily. We do not see Bond losing Honeychile, but in a later adventure, *The Man With the Golden Gun*, we learn that Honeychile marries and has two children.

Eco's list focuses attention on Bond's sexual relationship with the girl, the object of Bond's sexual desires—and, to the extent that readers identify with him, the object of the sexual desires of these readers. In the traditional fairy tale, this element of the story is not emphasized, though the hero and heroine do marry and live happily ever after.

Eco also provides a paradigmatic analysis of the typical Bond text. In these text we find the following oppositions (Table 9.1; I have modified the oppositions slightly, to make them more understandable):

MAKE YOUR OWN

AN EXOTICALLY NAMED SUPERVILLAIN

Le Gauche, a 500-pound gourmet with a penchant for cannibalism	Alec Borglum Scofflaw, notorious kingpin of S.E.R.E.N.D.I.P.I.T.Y. (The Special Executive for Revenge, Extortion, Nasty Looks, Dog-Kicking, Insults, Perversion, Impoliteness, Torture, and Yellow Journalism)	Dr. Wrongfinger, one-armed gynecologist who works sixteen hours a day to make up for lost time	Dingo Noir, who once wagered his wife against 400 pounds of uncut marzipan in a baccarat game, and lost	Rosa Scarab, ex-Wac general who wears a barbed-wire anklet and exercises by throwing Irish wolfhounds in front of trains

WITH HEADQUARTERS IN SOME EXOTIC SECRET LOCALE

Inside the left hind leg of the Sphinx	A giant submarine in an obscure Minnesota lake	A high-rise tree house in a Colombian rain forest	A marijuana plantation in northern California	A luxurious dirigible that circles Swiss banks and German girls' schools

ASSISTED BY AN EXOTICALLY NAMED AND UNIQUELY LETHAL HENCHMAN

Look See, whose piercing stare ignites underwear	Bedfellow, a pajama-wearing colossus whose crushing embrace is fatal	Loudmouth, whose vociferous yells curl all of the hair and break all of the glass within a twenty-mile radius	Bite Size, a midget who kicks tall men in the lap	Rock Bottom, who can deflect the most powerful blows with his buttocks

SETS OUT TO WREAK HAVOC ON THE WORLD WITH AN INGENIOUS PLAN

To kidnap the wife of the president of the United States and up-end her on network television	To airlift the entire population of New York City to Hollywood Boulevard	To pour the Great Lakes into the Grand Canyon to get the returnable bottles at their bottom	To stage a lesbian commando raid on the men's room of the U.S. Senate	To skywrite pornography above the Vatican

Figure 9.1. Formula for James Bond Movie. Reprinted by permission of Larry Tritten. © Larry Tritten.

JAMES BOND MOVIE

BY LARRY TRITTEN

BOND SEDUCES VARIOUS EXOTICALLY
NAMED WOMEN WITH THE OPPOSITION OR ON HIS SIDE

Flicka Barnstorm, Swedish aviatrix and nude skydiver with rip-cord burns on both nipples	Candy Hammer, stripper, centerfold model, and double agent for the Moral Majority	Edelschwarz Frisch, Jamaican-Swiss adventuress enamored of waterskiing wearing Ben Wa balls	Yummy Moussaka, Greek waitress skilled at serving dessert on all fours	Poontang Ersatz, New Orleans hooker and horizontal marital arts expert

AND ULTIMATELY SUCCEEDS
AFTER A HARROWING CLOSE CALL OR TWO

Riding a mechanical bull on Quaaludes	Rubbed with smelt and tossed into a leopard's cage	Forced to swim the English Channel after a smörgåsbord	Stuck with Crazy Glue to the leg of an elephant stampeded through a minefield	Without pants in an all-night theater in Times Square

WITH THE HELP
OF A SPECIAL WEAPON OR INVENTION

A plumber's helper tipped with curare	A remote-control chicken-sexing machine	A Mercedes with a trunkful of credit cards	A missile-firing hang glider	An ice-cycle (with blades instead of wheels) equipped with built-in crossbow

AS WE FADE OUT ON 007 AND
HIS SEXY COMPANION, BOND CAN BE HEARD TO SAY

"Come here, angel. I want to show you how to rub my stomach and pat my head at the same time."	"I think we've discovered a new erogenous zone, darling. Put your hands on your heels again, roll over slightly, and let me turn up the lamp!"	"Just pretend you're snorkeling, love ... but breathe through your nose and don't worry if the bed isn't big enough—I've put pillows on both sides."	"You vixen! Don't you know that ladies never bite when they kiss a gentleman below the waist?"	"I'm anything but shy, my love, but I'd rather put the monkey in the next room, if you don't mind."

According to Bennett and Woollacott, Eco "construes 'the girl' as a potential mediator between Bond and the villain" (p. 74). In the case of *Dr. No* I disagree. I think the basic polarity is between Honeychile/Honey and Dr. No/Guano and it is Bond who is the mediating figure. Putting the girl in between Bond and the villain privileges the girl and sexual relationships and though sexuality is important, and Bond can be interpreted as a hyperphallic hero, there are other relationships and aspects to the plot of *Dr. No* that are more significant. I am not sure that the basic opposition in all Bond stories is between Bond and some villain or that in genre narratives, in general, the opposition is always or even generally between the hero and the villain.

The qualities that Eco (1985) finds on the Bond part of the opposition does show how these stories reflect and reinforce an ideological position. Bond is a hero who reflects the values of the so-called free world and, in particular, England. Bennett and Woollacott discuss how, as the Bond books and films progressed, Bond evolved as a hero representing, in his various incarnations, such values as modernization, detente (with the Communist world), and even feminism (seen in the comedy tied to his sexuality).

Bond as a Mythic Hero

It should not be a surprise that there is a connection between heroes of modern popular culture and ancient myths, for it is in these myths that many of the prototypes of modern heroes and heroines are found.[1]

For one thing, ancient heroes were great adventurers, traveling all over the place in search of excitement. They also were often philanderers—they spent a good deal of time and energy, away from their wives, involved with early incarnations of "the girl." Odysseus, remember, spent a year with a beautiful sorceress, Circe. And Helen provided enormous complications for the Trojans and was ultimately the reason for the destruction of Troy. Hers was the face that "launched a thousand ships." Odysseus was also a resourceful and crafty person, who used his ingenuity to escape from difficult situations; Bond is like him in this respect, as well. In certain respects, then, both are "trickster" heroes, a universal kind of hero.

According to Holtsmark (as quoted in Lehr, 1988), one of the favorite themes of classical authors was to subject their heroes to a "journey through hell," a narrative pattern known as *katabasis* (Greek for going down). Holtsmark argues that this theme is found in texts such as *Miami Vice* (Sonny Crockett wandering through the seamy districts of South Florida) and *Apocalypse Now!* (Willard wandering through the jungles of Southeast Asia). We find this theme in *Dr. No*, when Bond escapes from his cell, plunges down the shaft designed to kill him, and wanders into the cavern where No is supervising the loading of Guano onto a ship.

These classical heroes had a helper, technically a *psychopompos* (escorter of souls to and from hell), who was traditionally Black. This was because this color is associated with the underworld, which is also black. In *Dr. No*, Quarrel, who helps Bond get to No's mysterious island, can be seen as a *psychopompos* and, significantly, is Black.

There are differences between mythic heroes and the typical heroes of folktales, as Bettelheim (1975) points out in his book *The Uses of Enchantment*. It may be that in popular literature, we find elements of both the folktale and the myth combining and that the widespread appeal of characters such as Bond and other popular heroes is connected to their having mythical dimensions that generate all kinds of meanings and deal with matters of which readers and viewers are not always aware. In this respect, let us consider the Oedipal aspects of *Dr. No*. This notion that there is an important Oedipal component to the Bond stories is also discussed in *Bond and Beyond* (Bennett & Woollacott, 1987).

Dr. No and the Oedipus Complex

Bennett and Woollacott (1987) bring the subject of the Oedipus complex up a number of times in their book. For example, in discussing the structure of the Bond narratives and the matter of

class, the relations between Bond and the girl and the matter of
nation and nationhood, they write that these topics work alongside
one another.

> Alongside but not separate from: the distinctive narrative and ideo-
> logical economy of the Bond novels consists in the way these two
> sources of narrative and ideological tension are imbricated on to and
> worked through in relation to one another. The means by which this
> overlapping is effected are supplied by the references to the Oedipus
> Complex which are present in all the novels. While these have usually
> been regarded as of a purely incidental significance—as either a crude
> means of titillating the reader, or as an over-obvious and heavy
> handed parody of the Oedipus myth—they in fact play an important
> part in organizing the narrative structure of the novels. (1987, p. 98)

In the case of *Dr. No*, it is No who represents the father figure—a
grotesque and powerful man with arcane knowledge who has
Bond and Honeychile in his power. Dr. Julius No's living room is
a huge room, lined on three sides with books. In a chapter titled
"Pandora Box," we read the following:

> Bond had assumed from the first that this man was a killer, that it
> would be a duel to the death. He had had his usual blind faith that
> he would win the duel—all the way until the moment when the
> flame-thrower had pointed at him. Then he had begun to doubt. Now
> he knew. This man was too strong, too well equipped. (Fleming, 1958,
> p. 134)

Later in the chapter, No tells Bond that he knows philosophy, he
knows ethics, he knows logic . . . better than Bond does. And in a
rather obvious reference to Oedipal concerns, No tells Bond something about his life and how he had been brought up with "no love"
and a "lack of parental care," how he had worked with Tongs.
"They represented," he explains, "revolt against the father figure
who had betrayed me."

Bond, himself, it can be argued, has suffered at the hands of a
father figure, M, who has symbolically castrated Bond at the beginning of the story—by depriving him of his gun and forcing him to
take a new weapon. No represents a rejection of his father and, he

adds, of all authority. Bond's triumph over Dr. No has, then, many different levels of significance. On one level, the psychological, Bond has bested a father figure and, only after that, is able to make love to Honeychile. And, on another level, he has shown that those who reject authority and the moral order (as represented by the free world) are doomed to failure. (No's passion, to turn bird dung into gold, also has psychoanalytic significance, but that topic is not germane to the analysis I am making here.)

Bond as a Hierarchical Elitist Hero

Using Aaron Wildavsky's typology, discussed earlier, it would seem reasonable to classify James Bond as a "hierarchical elitist" hero. He is one of a small group of spies who are licensed to kill. He works for an elite organization dedicated to maintaining the power relations that obtain in the world (including domination by the British and their allies), and he has a decidedly expensive lifestyle . . . paid for by the British government but, obviously, well worth the cost. A number of commentators have pointed out that Bond's taste is not really sophisticated but only seems to be (to people who do not know much about such things). He has his eccentricities—he likes his drinks shaken but not stirred, is very fastidious about the brands of wine and liquor he drinks, cigarettes he smokes, and presents an image of refined taste. But it is really more a middle class person's idea of what upper-class taste is than upper-class taste. An example of Bond requesting a drink in *Dr. No* follows: "I would like a medium Vodka dry Martini—with a slice of lemon peel. Shaken and not stirred, please. I would prefer Russian or Polish vodka" (1958, p. 131).

Dr. No, on the other hand, is a classic competitive individualist. He is out for himself, in essence. He accepts no authority and has big plans. He rules over a collection of people who seem close to what Wildavsky calls fatalists. They work for No, who seems to breed them to his own specifications. The Bond stories tend to have villains who are competitive individualists—though sometimes they are part of some organized terrorist collectivity.

TABLE 9.2 Four Ways of Analyzing Dr. No

Psychoanalytic	Semiotic	Marxist	Sociological
Oedipus complex	Propp	Ideology	Role of women
Symbolic castration	Lévi-Strauss	Bourgeois hero	Racism
Id/ego/superego	Artifacts	Chigroes/slaves	Uses of text
Scopophilia	Names used	Alienation	Gratifications
Oral/anal/phallic	No's signs	Patriarchy	Class

If there is an egalitarian figure in the story it would probably be Honeychile, a nature goddess, with little truck for civilized ways. She lives on the margins of society, though she has hopes of entering it some day. (In recent work, Wildavsky has added a fifth kind of person, a hermit—who has little to do with society and Honeychile actually seems to fit this designation best.)

Four Ways of Analyzing Dr. No

Let me conclude this discussion with a schematic suggestion (Table 9.2) of four ways (there are, of course, many others one might use) one can interpret Dr. No. Many of the topics listed here have been dealt with in this chapter and in the earlier discussions of the novel.

There are many different ways of interpreting Dr. No as Table 9.2 indicates—and a number of the topics suggest moving from one methodology to another. Let me cite one example: the psychoanalytic concept of scopophilia, which deals with the way we obtain sexual gratification by visual means, also is connected to the patriarchical sexuality found in the book—the pattern of male domination that informs Dr. No and all the Bond novels and films.

If James Bond is, as Bennett and Woollacott (1987) suggest, the most famous fictional hero of the last forty years, he demands and deserves our attention. In rather complex ways, people identify with heroes and heroines. It is the task of the analyst of media and genres to see how these heroes function in their stories and genres

and to consider what role the heroes may be playing and what
functions they may be serving in society.

Note

1. This analysis draws upon an essay by Jeff Lehr (1988). "Me Tarzan, You,
Odysseus: Classical Myth in Popular Culture," which first appeared in the *Iowa
Alumni Review*. The essay deals with the ideas of Jack Holtsmark, a classics professor
at the University of Iowa, author of *Tarzan and Tradition* which deals with mythology
and popular culture. Reprinted in Berger, 1991.

What elevates good SF above the rest is what separates all good literature from the mediocre: good plot, interesting characters, and that one quality which the good SF writer has in abundance—a high degree of creative insight. . . . We sometimes forget that the SF writer lives, as we do, in the now of his existence. While he writes of the future, he also has his feet planted on his cultural *terra firma*, and he is making a statement about the present. When the SF writer sits down to spin his fictional web, he is drawing upon current ideas, technology, and trends; through extrapolation and projection he shows us another tomorrow.

SOURCE: Hollister, B. C. (Ed.). (1974). *Another tomorrow: A science fiction anthology*. Dayton, OH: Pflaum Publishing.

10

War of the Worlds

In this chapter I analyze one of the recognized classics of science fiction, *War of the Worlds*. I also deal with the nature of the genre, with the significance of aliens in the public mind, with Susan Sontag's (1965) well-known essay on the formulaic aspects of science fiction (it is reprinted in many anthologies on the subject), and with the radio dramatization of the novel by Orson Welles, which led to a huge panic in America.

War of the Worlds: A Synopsis

Strange metallic cylindrical vehicles from Mars suddenly land on the earth, in England. They are inhabited by Martians, beings that, it turns out, have evolved much further than humans and are essentially nonhumanoid. In Mars they developed to the point where now they are essentially all brain (emotionless, inhabiting a disgusting body with tentacles), live in a germ free environment and maintain themselves, vampirelike, by drinking blood directly from the veins of their victims. They erect devices that allow them to be ambulatory and start destroying everything in their path. The story is told by an unnamed narrator, who is an on the scene observer and who, at various points, finds himself teamed up with a weak-willed curate and an artilleryman with the will to struggle on (in subterranean areas, away from the Martians) and, it turns out, delusions of grandeur. There are fierce battles waged against the Martians, who have infinitely superior technology. They have a lethal death ray and use what we now would call poison gas. They are on the point of developing flying devices (which means they can take over the world). It looks like the Martians will be invincible but suddenly they stop fighting, having fallen victim to microbes, which are alien to their experience in that they lived in a germ-free environment on Mars.

Speculations on the Nature of Science Fiction and Its Subgenres

The other genres I have dealt with in these chapters on specific texts are pretty easily defined, so I have not discussed, in any great detail, their characteristics. With science fiction, however, the situation is different. There is a considerable amount of controversy about what science fiction is. Obviously we are dealing with texts (my focus here will be on novels, but science fiction is a very important film genre) that involve science, somehow, and are fictions, or fabricated stories. But science fiction is to a great degree, it would seem, about human courage, about relationships among people, about resoluteness in the face of danger, about human curiosity about the unknown, and science is only a factor in these texts.

Some analysts, who are very latitudinarian, see science fiction as having a number of subcategories or subgenres, covering everything from bug-eyed monsters (BEMS) to sword and sorcery stories and fantasy fiction (horror, gothic stories, ghost stories, etc.). Others tend to restrict science fiction to stories about aliens, time travel, space travel (known often as "space operas"), utopias and dystopias, and the investigation of unknown worlds. Some might add postcatastrophe adventures. And one could find other subgenres, no doubt.

TABLE 10.1 Science Fiction Genres and Important Texts

Aliens	Time Travel	Space Travel	Utopia/Dystopia
Wells, *War of the Worlds*	Wells, *The Time Machine*	Clarke, *A Space Odyssey*	Zamiatin, *We*

Unknown Worlds	Postcatastrophe	Sword & Sorcery	Alternative History
Herbert, *Dune*	Miller, *A Canticle for Liebowitz*	Howard, *Conan: The Barbarian*	Dick, *The Man in the High Castle*

In Table 10.1, I list some of the more important subgenres of science fiction and suggest a significant text for each category.

The matter is complicated because there are often mixtures in which we have, for example, aliens and space travel or time travel and unknown worlds. There is also the question of whether science fiction, as a genre literature, is popular culture or fine art. After all, science fiction covers everything from comic book heroes (Superman is, remember, an alien) to work by distinguished novelists such as Vladimir Nabokov, Jorge Luis Borges, Doris Lessing, and Ursula Le Guin.

Let me offer a couple of characterizations of science fiction before I start my analysis of *War of the Worlds*—a text that just about everyone agrees is a classic work of science fiction. In the introduction to *Science Fiction: The Future*, Dick Allen (1971) writes that

> the old science fiction was a type of literature that stressed the future and made new inventions seem plausible—in some ways it was a literature of translation. The scientists came up with various hypothetical inventions and the SF writers wove stories around these inventions. Science fiction was (a large part of it still is) that genre of literature defined by SF writer and critic Sam Moskowitz as "a branch of fantasy identifiable by the fact that it eases the 'willing suspension of disbelief' on the part of its readers by utilizing an atmosphere of scientific credibility for its imaginative speculations in physical science, time, social science and philosophy." (p. 1)

Allen suggests that the best way to describe new science fiction is
that it has moved from speculations about scientific inventions to
speculations about how human beings react to "future shock." He
sees science fiction as a popular form of the epic, with larger-than-
life heroes whose basic motivations are quest and self-discovery.

In these stories, humans make a difference. Their struggles are
internal (with themselves) and external (with dangerous beings,
new problems, etc.) The plots are strong, characterization is very
important, and there is a good deal of action as heroes and heroines
continually face new and unexpected threats and dangers. There
are often philosophical and religious underpinnings in these stories, for as the protagonists explore, for example, outer space, they
are drawn to musing about such things as the nature of mortality,
the possibility of afterlife, and the existence of God (or some force
that is behind everything).

In an excellent survey of science fiction, *The Visual Encyclopedia
of Science Fiction*, George Turner (1977) discusses "Science Fiction
as Literature," and he defines science fiction as follows:

> Modern science fiction scours science, art and philosophy for alter-
> native possibilities of living, of action, of seeing, thinking and desir-
> ing. When it explores these possibilities with such logic as the writer
> can bring to bear, without succumbing to the transparent escapism of
> fantasy, science fiction serves a purpose outside the common limits
> of realistic fiction. So it seems reasonable to this writer to categorise
> science fiction as the literature of possible alternatives. (p. 257)

This notion of alternatives causes a radical shift in the structuring
of stories from a focus on characters as the source of action to the
environment and external factors, Turner adds.

This tends to push science fiction in the direction of "thrillers"
and has caused some critics to attack science fiction for not having
adequately developed characters. Turner argues that science fiction
can have good characterization and, in effect, that it is the quality
of the novelist, not the genre, that determines the quality of the text.
The distinctive technical problem of science fiction—the matter of
alternative possibilities—is an innovation basic to the genre and

does not, in any way, limit the ability of a good author to create memorable characters and first class novels.

Alien Invaders

Let us turn, now, to our text—*War of the Worlds*. It was written in 1897 and is one of the earliest science fiction novels. The first paragraph of the book is beautifully written and crucially important. Let me quote it and discuss it.

No one would have believed in the last years of the nineteenth century that this world was being watched keenly and closely by intelligences greater than man's and yet as mortal as his own; that as men busied themselves about their various concerns they were being scrutinized and studied, perhaps almost as narrowly as a man with a microscope might scrutinize the transient creatures that swarm and multiply in a drop of water. With infinite complacency men went to and fro over this globe about their little affairs, serene in their assurance of their empire over matter. It is possible that the infusoria under the microscope do the same. No one gave a thought to the older worlds of space as sources of human danger, or thought of them only to dismiss the idea of life upon them as impossible or improbable. It is curious to recall some of the mental habits of those departed days. At most, terrestrial men fancied there might be other men on Mars, perhaps inferior to themselves and ready to welcome a missionary enterprise. Yet across the gulf of space, minds that are to our minds as ours are to those of the beasts that perish, intellects vast and cool and unsympathetic, regarded this earth with envious eyes, and slowly and surely drew their plans against us. And early in the twentieth century came the great disillusionment. (Wells, 1964, p. 1)

Notice how beautifully Wells sets the scene. Human beings are going about their daily tasks without any sense of the danger that they are in, "serene" in their sense that they were the center of the universe, "serene in their assurance of their empire over matter." It is possible, Wells speculates, that infusoria in a drop of water also feel that they are at the center of things. This serenity would, of course, soon be shattered.

These innocent earthlings, it turns out, are being studied by creatures of vast and prodigious intelligence. Various analogies are used by Wells. First, human beings are being studied by Martians the same way that we use a microscope to study microbes in a drop of water. (These microbes, which will be our salvation, are introduced in the very first paragraph.) Second, Martians have minds that are to human minds as human minds are to those of "beasts that perish." The Martians, it turns out, herd human beings, for their blood, just the way humans herd beasts, for their meat and milk. Let me show these analogies in a diagrammatic form:

Human Beings : Martians as Microbes : Human Beings	Martian Minds : Human Minds as Human Minds : Animal Minds

These analogies are chilling.

What makes things worse is that these intellects are not only vast but also "cool and unsympathetic." They regard us, for example, the same way we regard microbes. There is, Wells suggests, a kind of purely logical intelligence at work, though how pure intelligence could be envious (which seems to imply emotion) is somewhat of a problem.

The "great disillusionment" involves our discovery that we are not alone in the universe and that we, most certainly, are not supreme in it. Our notion that we had "empire over matter" was dashed. The creatures from Mars, Wells writes, on just the second page of the book, evolved into their form due to the pressures of necessity. It had, he says, "brightened their intellects, enlarged their powers, and hardened their hearts." These Martians, living on a dying planet, looked across space and saw the earth, "green with vegetation and grey with water." And he points out, humans must be to the Martians "at least as alien and lowly as are the monkeys and lemurs to us." (1964, p. 8)

In this analogy, we are raised up from microbes to the status of monkeys and lemurs, creatures that are relatively close to humans on the evolutionary scale. We can add another analogy to our diagram:

> Martians : Humans as
> Humans : Monkeys and Lemurs

This device, of using analogies, does a beautiful job of establishing, in very graphic ways, the differences between the Martians and humans and explaining the behavior of Martians.

The Martians, as Wells describes them, are physically disgusting:

> They were huge round bodies—or rather, heads—about four feet in diameter, each body having in front of it a face. This face had no nostrils—indeed the Martians do not seem to have had any sense of smell, but it had a pair of very large dark-coloured eyes, and just beneath this a kind of fleshy beak. . . . In a group round the mouth were sixteen slender, almost whip-like tentacles, arranged in two bunches of eight each. (1964, p. 111)

He adds later that "they were heads—merely heads. Entrails they had none. They did not eat, much less digest. Instead, they took the fresh, living blood of other creatures, and *injected* it into their own veins" (p. 112). He tells us later that these creatures were lifted above "organic fluctuations of mood and emotion" and did not sleep, had no sense of fatigue and were "absolutely without sex." That had become, he tells us, "mere selfish intelligence, without any of the emotional substratum of the human being" (1964, p. 114).

Wells establishes the problems created in stories about aliens. They have, generally speaking, incredible power and great intelligence, but they have no emotions, no sense of empathy with others. They are, then, *inhuman*. (The term *alien* means, literally, no ties, no connections.)

In the novel we find a set of oppositions established between humans and Martians (Table 10.2). The narrator, a scientifically minded observer, more or less mediates between these two polarities. He is, of course, human and subject to human frailties, but he also, by chance, finds himself trapped in a house where he can observe the Martians in considerable detail.

In *War of the Worlds* we find two other important characters, a curate and an artilleryman. The narrator spends time with each of

TABLE 10.2 Oppositions Between Humans and Martians

Martians	Humans
Intelligence, no emotion	Emotions, feelings, intelligence
Asexual	Sexual
Mind	Body
Technologically advanced	Technologically primitive
Powerful	Weak
Calculating	Unsuspecting

them. He is, it turns out, forced to kill the curate, who is in the house with him near the Martians. The curate collapses under the strain of events and believes the end of the world is at hand. He starts shouting and has to be silenced. The artilleryman, on the other hand, has grandiose plans about taking humanity underground, and fighting against the Martians. The artilleryman has been digging a hole to reach a huge drain. When the narrator looks at it, he realizes the gulf between the artilleryman's dreams and his powers.

Aliens as Viruses

Stories about aliens invading the earth are, I would suggest, metaphors that relate to our feelings and anxieties about the human body being invaded by germs and diseases. These diseases often seem to have a kind of intelligence; they, somehow, foil our efforts to repel them, they frequently attack our blood and are repelled by mechanisms in our blood, as well. In some cases, they kill us— destroying themselves, of course, at the same time. They are too ignorant to realize that. (Some parasites, on the other hand, seem to have enough wit to merely use us as a source of life without killing us.)

These viruses, microbes, whatever, are strangers in a strange land (to them) that have mysterious powers and, almost always, are dangerous and life-threatening. They are, also, easy to hate and, we tend to feel, deserve to be destroyed. They provide us the same feelings, when we destroy them, as we feel when we kill a mosquito that is bothering us or some other insect. In science fiction, these alien beings take on all kinds of different forms: some are animal (like the monstrous beings from Mars), some are robots (with great power and intelligence), and some have the ability to change form, making them even more difficult to deal with. They are superior in certain respects, but always have some weakness, which human beings find (discovering the weakness in time to save the world, etc. is often a source of the excitement and drama) and use to destroy or neutralize them.

The New Aliens as Threats
to the Social Order

On the social and political level, these beings represent a fear of foreigners, anxiety about contamination of national values, racial purity and related concerns. The aliens, in this case, are people from different countries with different values, different beliefs, different religions, who pose a threat to our way of life, which is, of course, the "right" way. They also seem to be particularly attracted to our women, and thus pose a threat to our racial purity and a threat to our sense of potency or adequacy as sexual beings.

In America, there has been a great deal of anxiety (and turmoil) throughout our history about immigration. We now seem to be reconciled to being a multicultural, multiracial society, but there is still widespread hostility, felt by many people, about immigrants, especially in that many of them actively compete with so-called American workers, most of whom come from families of earlier immigrants.

In the 1990s, there is now a widespread anxiety in first world countries (North America, Europe) about being "invaded" by people from second world countries (Russia, eastern Europe) and third world countries (Africa, Asia). Science fiction stories about aliens help us deal (at the unconscious level) with anxieties we feel about immigrants with alien cultures. In the stories, at least, we can zap the aliens and get rid of them. If my hypothesis about science fiction stories featuring aliens is correct, one would expect more novels and films about aliens to be created as the threat of invasion by aliens grows stronger.

Susan Sontag on the
Science Fiction Formula

Susan Sontag, a distinguished critic and social thinker, has written an influential article about the formulaic aspects of science fiction films. Her essay, "The Imagination of Disaster," (1965) makes light of the genre, suggesting it is so formulaic that it is uninteresting and that it provides "an inadequate response" to the terrors that we face. Her essay was written in 1965, so if it is somewhat dated and inaccurate, we must keep that in mind.

She sketches out the basic scenario of science fiction films as follows. I have slightly modified her formulations.

1. A thing arrives. Alien monsters emerge from a spaceship.
2. A hero reports great destruction caused by aliens, which is confirmed.
3. Conferences between the military and scientists take place.
4. Further atrocities are committed by the alien invaders.
5. More conferences trying to discover some vulnerability in the aliens. The hero is shown working in his lab, feverishly, developing something to destroy the aliens. They are repulsed but the question remains, "Have we seen the last of them?"

She also offers another version, for black-and-white "cheapie" films.

1. The hero and his girl friend (or family, if he's married) are someplace when strange things start happening. Plants become gigantic and ambulatory or someone starts acting very strangely.
2. The hero tries to warn the authorities, who do not believe him.
3. The hero consults others who are useless. Meanwhile, the thing (or whatever) is beginning to claim other victims.
4. The hero either finds a way to destroy the alien presence or convinces the authorities, who figure out a way to solve the problem.

Sontag mentions several other subgenres: the laboratory experiment that goes awry, the alteration of conditions accidently caused by nuclear testing (that will lead to the destruction of all life), and the space voyage. She admits that there are thousands of science fiction novels ("their heyday was the late 1940s") but says she wants to write about science fiction films because they provide "sensuous elaboration," or, to put it more directly, images and sounds that do not, like words, have to be translated into the imagination.

What science fiction films are about, she contends, is disaster. "Science fiction films are not about science. They are about disaster, which is one of the oldest subjects of art" (reprinted in Allen, 1971, p. 314). They deal with "the aesthetics of destruction, with the peculiar beauties to be found in wreaking havoc, making a mess." And their peculiar strength, she adds, is in creating the imagery of destruction.

The problem with science fiction films, she suggests, is that they are too simplistic, they put too much focus on "things, objects and machinery" instead of people, and though they are often highly moralistic, their focus on the "imagery of disaster" is an "inadequate response" to the problems human beings face in the 20th century. She is not averse to making sweeping generalizations. She writes that

> there is absolutely no social criticism, of even the most implicit kind, in science fiction films. No criticism, for example, of the conditions of our society which create the impersonality and dehumanization which science fiction fantasies displace onto the influence of an alien It. Also, the notion of science as a social activity, interlocking with social and political interests, is unacknowledged. Science is simply either adventure (for good or evil) or a technical response to danger. (reprinted in Allen, 1971, p. 322)

This statement, I suggest, is preposterous. She has even suggested, in one of her scenarios, that in some films we find competent authorities developing a technology to repel invaders. This suggests that science is, in certain ways, at the very least a "social" activity that also has a political dimension to it.

There is no question that she is correct in criticizing many of essentially mindless science fiction films that have been made. (She does not appreciate the social criticism in *King Kong*, seeing it, instead, as just another monster film.) But she is wrong in suggesting that science fiction films have no social dimensions to them (either direct or implied criticism), being instead, generally full of "wishful thinking." She sees these films as a kind of innocent escapism that like most popular culture, or so she asserts, distracts us and, even worse, gives us a false sense of security.

Most critics of science fiction make the opposite point about its relation to social and political concerns. Science fiction, they suggest, is so much involved with these matters, with alternative possibilities for social, political, economic, and even sexual arrangements that it does not develop its characters adequately.

It would be interesting to know what Sontag would write about science fiction films since 1965. I would imagine that it would be very difficult for her to make the same generalizations about the social dimensions of science fiction, or popular culture in general.

The Orson Welles Radio Broadcast

I will conclude this discussion of *War of the Worlds* with a brief discussion of a panic caused by a radio dramatization of the novel by Orson Welles on Halloween night, 1938. This subject was dealt with in a classic work of social science, Hadley Cantril's *The Invasion From Mars: A Study in the Psychology of a Panic*. Cantril (1966) estimated that six million people heard the broadcast and that one million of them were frightened or disturbed.

People who tuned in late (and even some who listened from the beginning) thought they heard a news report about Martians landing in New Jersey and destroying everything. Some listeners kept a cool head, recognizing they were listening to a radio dramatization, but others panicked, fleeing their homes, seeking out priests for final confessions, and so forth. Cantril characterized this panic as follows:

Granted that some people believed the broadcast to be true, why did they become so hysterical? Why did they pray, telephone relatives, drive at dangerous speeds, cry, awaken sleeping children and flee? (1966, p. 197)

Because, he adds, people actually believed their safety was at stake. When this happens, panic breaks out.

The matter was complicated, because the behavior of the individuals who panicked was connected to social forces. As Cantril writes:

There is every reason to believe that the anxiety and fear revealed by the panic were latent in the general population, not specific to the persons who happened to participate in it. (p. 202)

At the time of the broadcast, the political situation was scary and, most importantly, the country had been in a severe depression for a decade. People were frustrated and anxious and thus susceptible to panic. The broadcast, available on records, was also brilliantly done, with a superb cast. This probably contributed somewhat to the impact of the show.

The actual form of the program—a music show that was interrupted for important news—was one that the radio audience was familiar with. Interruptions for important breaking news are an aspect of news programs and these interruptions had the effect, for those who did not listen carefully to the statements about the show being a dramatization (and took no note of the fact that the show was being broadcast Halloween night), of turning the music show into a news show, of overriding some people's doubts and credulity and convincing them that the earth actually was being invaded by Martians. The panic of October 30, 1938, can be seen as an example of genre confusion—certain elements of the population mistook a radio dramatization of a well-known science fiction novel for a news story.

The broadcast fed on the anxiety in many people about the Germans and the Japanese, though as Cantril points out:

To imply that specific events that recently occurred in Europe and were broadcast to the United States served as the chief cause of the panic would be to disregard the multitude of other factors we have found so important. (pp. 202-203)

The troubling events in Europe, Cantril suggests, played a part in the panic but were not the most important causes of it.

Conclusions

The War of the Worlds is a science fiction classic that speaks to our fears and anxieties about our safety and our place in the cosmos. Science fiction novels often involve the survival of the world in the face of some alien invaders or scientific or natural catastrophe. Novels like *War of the Worlds* speak to our hidden fears and anxieties and give us hope that there is, ultimately, a reason to be confident about our ability to survive, at the very least.

As the narrator explains in the final chapter:

We have learned that we cannot regard this planet as being fenced in and a secure abiding-place for Man; we can never anticipate the unseen good or evil that may come upon us suddenly from out of space. It may be that in the larger design of the universe this invasion from Mars is not without its ultimate benefit for men; it has robbed us of that serene confidence in the future which is the most fruitful source of decadence, the gifts to human science it has brought are enormous, and it has done much to promote the conception of the commonweal of mankind. (Wells, 1964, p. 159)

We have learned a great deal from this experience, our narrator tells us, and though the destruction caused by the Martians was awesome, we have also benefitted immensely in terms of our scientific and political development. The threats posed from outer space have taught us, at the very least, that we must learn to live with one another on earth.

It is interesting to notice that science fiction is becoming increasingly important in films in the 1990s. The most expensive and probably the most important film of the Summer of 1991 was *The*

Terminator II, advertised now as "*T-2*", a 100 million dollar (approximately) sequel, with incredible special effects, to *The Terminator*, a low-budget (six million dollar) film made in 1984. (The original *Terminator* is analyzed in my *Agitpop: Political Culture and Communication Theory*, 1990.)

Science fiction is a genre that enables film makers to use all kinds of remarkable special effects and create texts that television cannot duplicate. Made-for-television films (and television programs) cannot afford the special effects used in films and the impact of these effects on the small television screen is not as great as it is in films, which are shown on enormous screens and have excellent sound, as well. Given the success of *The Terminator II*, it is likely that science fiction will become increasingly important as a film genre and that audiences will find themselves watching increasingly menacing cyborgs, robots and aliens, on earth and in outer space.

Mary Shelley's *Frankenstein* is a very bookish book, permeated with literary allusions, quotations, references and parallels. From what might have been a literary *olla podrida* [originally a Spanish stew of meat and vegetables but now used to suggest a mixture of various elements] of Romantic themes and types, however, the firm mind of the author has finally drawn a coherent thematic pattern worthy of serious regard. Two great literary sources stand behind this pattern, it seems to me, the Faust myth and Milton's *Paradise Lost*. These . . . intermingle to the extent that the various actions of the romance—those involving Frankenstein and Walton, on the one hand, and that of the Monster on the other—can all be said to raise questions of the relationship of man to God, or nature, or more narrowly, of universal law or justice.

SOURCE: Mays, M. A. (1971, p. 171) *Frankenstein*: Mary Shelley's Black Theodicy. In Thomas D. Clareson (Ed.), *SF: The Other Side of Realism: Essays on Modern Fantasy and Science Fiction*. Bowling Green University Popular Press.

11

Frankenstein: The New Prometheus

The Creation of the Novel

The details involving the creation of the book, *Frankenstein,* are almost as incredible as the creation of the central character of the book. The being created by Dr. Victor Frankenstein and commonly known as Frankenstein most certainly is one of the most famous creatures, monsters, nightmare figures—call him or it what you will—in all literature, a figure who has a remarkable hold on our imaginations. (Although unnamed in the book, the monster has come, in popular usage, to be known as Frankenstein. Thus we have films with titles such as *Bride of Frankenstein* that adopt this convention.)

Why the monster is so resonant is something of an enigma. The quotation by Mays refers to the Faust myth and to Milton's *Paradise Lost,* which deal with, among other things, our desire for immortality. In Paradise, Adam and Eve were immortal; it was only after they tasted of the tree of knowledge that they were expelled and became mortal.

Frankenstein was written by Mary Shelley, a nineteen-year-old woman, at the suggestion of the poet Byron. Byron proposed that he, Shelley (a famous poet), Shelley's wife, and a friend, a Dr. Polidori, amuse themselves by each writing a "macabre" story to help pass the time during a summer they were all spending together in Switzerland. The book was published in 1818, which means that Dr. Frankenstein's monster has been scaring the devil out of people for more than 170 years. Mary Shelley described what was on her mind in creating the book in a preface she wrote to the 1831 edition.

I busied myself *to think of a story* . . . which would speak to the mysterious fears of our nature, and awaken thrilling horror—one to make the reader dread to look round, to curdle the blood and quicken the beatings of the heart. (1967, p. v)

Her words speak very graphically to one of the main functions of horror literature—to provide thrills and to scare people by connecting to various morbid residues in our psyches.

The Creation of the Monster

Why is it that Frankenstein's monster has become so important a figure? Why is it that he dominates our imagination so powerfully? What is it that gives this gigantic, eight-foot figure, created out of dead flesh and yet alive, so much cultural resonance?

The monster is a figure who mediates between dominant oppositions in the book and in the human mind—between life and death. Frankenstein's monster is dead flesh that, somehow, is given the spark of life and, as such, a creature that transcends life and death.

As the monster's creator, Dr. Frankenstein says, in describing his feelings about the creature:

No one can conceive of the variety of feelings which bore me onwards, like a hurricane, in the first enthusiasm of success. Life and death appeared to me ideal bounds, which I should first break through, and pour a torrent of light into our dark world. A new species would bless me as its creator and source; many happy and excellent natures would owe their being to me. No father could claim the gratitude of his child so completely as I should deserve theirs. Pursuing these reflections,

> I thought that if I could bestow animation upon lifeless matter, I might
> in process of time . . . renew life where death had apparently devoted
> the body to corruption. (1967, pp. 38, 39)

There is a tragic irony in the story for Frankenstein's creation
becomes a monster who kills everyone his creator loves and wreaks
havoc on a world that abhors and shuns him.

Frankenstein's creation turns out to be a monster, it might be
argued, by chance and a decent case might be made that he is, in
reality, an heroic figure who is driven to commit his crimes by a
sense of rejection and alienation. To the extent that he is dead flesh
come alive in a world where that never happens, he is one more
alien figure from the world of science fiction, which is one reason,
as I suggested in my chapter on this subject, some critics see horror
as a subgenre of science fiction.[1]

The monster is repudiated by everyone because he is unnatural,
because he inspires revulsion, representing as he does the violation
of divine law, which tells us that man must not create life, that we
must not tamper with natural processes in this area, and that if we
do, things will turn out terribly.

The monster, we must remember, did not create himself. In a
sense, he is the victim of Dr. Frankenstein's transgressions—of
society's inability to see this creature as a new Adam. Thus the
monster is justified, in a sense, when he pleads with Dr. Frankenstein, his creator, for understanding.

> Oh, Frankenstein, be not equitable to every other and trample upon
> me alone, to whom thy justice, and even they clemency and affection
> is most due. Remember that I am thy creature; and I ought to be thy
> Adam, but I am rather the fallen angel who thou drivest from joy for
> no misdeed. Everywhere I see bliss, from which I alone am irrevo-
> cably excluded. I was benevolent and good; misery made me a fiend.
> Make me happy, and I shall again be virtuous. (1967, p. 84)

This and various other entreaties Frankenstein's creation makes
fall on deaf ears and, as a result, he turns against his creator and
everyone else. He is, I would argue, as much a victim as a monster,

and his definition of himself as "monster" is one that society places upon him and which, ultimately, he comes to accept.

His monsterhood raises an interesting question. What is a monster? From a sociological perspective, one must be labeled a monster and treated as one by others to be confirmed in one's role. In his case, it was the sins of his creator, Dr. Frankenstein, that were visited upon him that led to his becoming a monster and, once confirmed as such, acting accordingly.

Oppositions in the Novel

The selections I have quoted establish the nature of the story. There is a binary opposition that informs the novel—the opposition between life and death. The monster transcends them, and this gives him an anxiety-provoking status. Human beings, we know, are either alive or dead. They are born, live, and die. Frankenstein is something that, somehow, is dead and yet alive, a creature who is the result of meddling by his creator in "realms reserved for God." The monster violates the logical exclusions, alive or dead, and reflecting our deepest fears and anxieties, escapes the control of his creator.

In the natural realm, control is not too great a problem, for all living things eventually die. But what do we do with monsters who are dead, yet somewhat alive? Let us look at this life versus death polarity and the extensions that come from it (Table 11.1).

These two oppositions reflect the boundaries within which human beings live. The monster's role, however, was to destroy these boundaries in that he represented both life and death, which is reflected in Table 11.2.

The monster, created from parts of dead bodies, is lifeless matter that somehow, magically, becomes animated. He is not the result of sexual relations between two human beings, the development of an egg into an embryo and the embryo into human form, but is, instead, the result of perverted knowledge, intruding into bounds

TABLE 11.1 Life and Death Polarities

Life	Death
Creation (sex)	Destruction
Naturally born	Naturally died
Growth	Decay
Change	Permanence
Controlled by man (social animal)	Controlled by God (the soul)
Outside: light, air, sun	Inside: dark, putrid
Unitary: from an embryo	Decomposition
Feeling	Insensate

beyond man's understanding. Dr. Frankenstein, in a sense, can be seen as challenging God and the natural forces of the universe, and suffers grievously for his transgressions.

The novel is informed by irony. Dr. Frankenstein's creation is not his Adam, but, instead, a fallen angel—in part because of Victor Frankenstein refusal to make a companion for his creation. Instead of a "new species to bless its creator," Dr. Frankenstein produces the instrument of his own destruction.

On Monsters and the Psyche

One of the reasons creatures like Frankenstein's monster and other monsters excite and intrigue people is because they wonder what it would be like to be "out of control" the ways monsters are—to escape from all the inhibitions society places upon us and, somehow, let ourselves go and do whatever we want to do. Most of us have strong super-egos that inhibit us, but the idea of being powerful, of allowing our impulses free reign, appeals to us while, at the same time, it frightens us.

In *The Strategy of Desire*, Ernest Dichter (a psychologist who developed the science of motivation research for advertisers) makes some interesting points about how people react to monsters. He argues that

TABLE 11.2 Life Versus Monster Polarity

Life	Monster (Life and Death)
Naturally born	Unnaturally born
Created from living body	Created from dead flesh
Insider: accepted	Outsider: rejected
Sex good: life from life	Sex bad: cannot have life from death
Live but slowly dying	Dead but living
Natural human form	Unnatural human form
Lives in society	Solitary, alien figure
Controlled by society	Not controlled by society
Good	Evil
Outside world: sun, air	Inside world: laboratory, darkness
Beautiful	Ugly

the inability of society to act quickly to control these monsters is really a consequence of society's own guilt. And this guilt is the result of four factors:

1. A feeling of sharing the responsibility for the creations of these creatures.
2. An expression of a failure to act on the recognition of the essential humanity of these creatures.
3. The feeling that "there, but for the grace of God, go I."
4. Society's recognition of the monster in itself. "How like myself that monster really is." (1960, pp. 196, 197)

One of the problems these monsters create for us is that we do not know where to locate the evil. Is the monster in the creator of the monster or in the monster himself? We solve this problem, Dichter suggests, by having the monster go out of control, thus locating the evil in the monster and making it acceptable to do away with him.

We can attack the monster and experience a kind of guilt-free aggression against an obviously horrible creature that needs to be destroyed. We do not blame Dr. Frankenstein (or the creators of other monsters) for creating someone or something that can go out of control; instead, we blame the monsters, who can be seen, in this respect, as victims of their creators and society. In this regard, consider the monster's touching entreaty to his creator.

Believe me, Frankenstein, I was benevolent; my soul glowed with love and humanity; but am I not alone, miserably alone? You, my creator, abhor me; what hope can I gather from your fellow creatures, who owe me nothing? They spurn and hate me. . . . Shall I not then hate them who abhor me? I will keep no terms with my enemies. (1967, p. 84)

But Victor Frankenstein shows no *compassion*, the word used by his creation, who then becomes a destructive monster.

On the Psychology of Horror

The oppositions found in *Frankenstein* provide insights into the nature of horror. The book is a classic horror story, which was written for one basic purpose—to scare people. But what is horror? Mary Shelley offers us some insights in her description of a nightmare she had, which, she tells us, led to the creation of the book. She writes:

I saw—with shut eyes, but acute mental vision—I saw the pale student of unhallowed arts kneeling beside the thing he had put together. I saw the hideous phantasm of a man stretched out, and then, on the working of some powerful engine, show signs of life and stir with an uneasy, half-vital motion. Frightful must it be, for supremely frightful would be the effect of any human endeavor to mock the stupendous mechanism of the Creator of the world. His success would terrify the artist; he would rush away from his odious handwork, horror-stricken. (1967, p. xv)

One aspect of horror, from Mary Shelley's perspective, is ugliness and the grotesque. Horror is also connected with nightmare visions of something dead that, somehow, lives—something that has power but no humanity. The monster, who escapes Dr. Frankenstein's control, is really a mirror of him, for he has searched for knowledge beyond human boundaries and, in that respect, escaped the control of God. Dr. Frankenstein's hubris is reflected in his monster's destructiveness.

Horror is different from terror, which we may describe as an extreme form of fear. Horror involves something more diffuse, a sense of anxiety and dread, tied to the unknown. The significance of the monster is that he (it?) calls forth latent, submerged, morbid, unconscious anxieties in people—he is a nightmare creature who speaks to our secret fears and evokes dread, disgust, fright, and similar feelings in us.

There is, I should point out, a strong Oedipal element in the story (though in a somewhat unnatural form). *Frankenstein* is, after all, a story about a "son" who destroys his "father" (we can substitute creature and creator here). And like the child who must be socialized, must learn language and customs, the monster, a new Prometheus, undergoes the same process of development. When first created, the creature is mute and ignorant. By chance, he has the good fortune to be able to observe a family and gain knowledge about mankind and society, and his development mirrors the development of children, with one major difference. He learns purely by observation, not being able to participate in society.

He is an Adamic figure and he becomes society's stepchild, driven by his terrible loneliness to revenge. "I am miserable," the monster tells his creator, pleading with him for a partner to share his loneliness, "and they shall share my wretchedness." Then he adds, pleading with Dr. Frankenstein:

> Yet it is in your power to recompense me and deliver them from an evil which it only remains for you to make so great, that not only you and your family, but thousands of others, shall be swallowed up in the whirlwinds of its rage. (1967, p. 84)

The monster was not created as an evil thing and was not an evil being at first. He became evil because he was rejected by his creator, shunned by society and denied the one favor he asked—a partner with whom to live so as to avoid what is suggested to be the worst of all curses, loneliness.

Conclusions

The monster, who in popular usage bears his creator's name, is a symbol of incredible resonance. Our interest in horror may reflect our fascination with the mysteries of creation at a time when traditional religions are losing their appeal for many people. In a sense, horror might be seen as a functional alternative to traditional religion (and a reversal of many of its values). *Frankenstein* (and texts in the horror genre) may be seen as a symbol of our desire to escape from the confines of human rationality, a "normal" life and the numerous burdens and limitations that society imposes on us.

The story is also a parable about the evolution of humanity and a warning about the danger of overreaching knowledge. Part of the monster's power, as a symbolic figure, probably stems from the strong Oedipal component of the story—a son who kills (by breaking his heart) his father and all those he loves, and in a vengeance driven fury, wreaks terror on society—until, as the book concludes, he leaps upon a raft of ice that is borne away by waves "and lost in darkness and distance" (1967, p. 206).

From a Freudian psychoanalytic perspective, there may also be an element of castration anxiety (and other disguised and perhaps repressed sexual aspects) to horror stories—that scare the hell out of people (and in films generate almost hysterical screaming at times) yet are eventually resolved in an acceptable manner, with the triumph of good over evil. Whatever the case, horror stories have a curious appeal to us and represent one of the most popular genres of books and films, for reasons which I hope I have helped, to some measure, explain.

Note

1. In the introduction to the Bantam edition of the book, Robert Donald Spector makes this point. He argues that *Frankenstein* ties the gothic romance to modern science and created a "robot" book. (See Scholes, 1967.)

Dealing with any text belonging to "literature," we must take into account a double requirement. First, we must be aware that it manifests properties that it shares with all literary texts, or with texts belong to one of the sub-groups of literature (which we call, precisely, genres). It is inconceivable, nowadays, to defend the thesis that everything in a work is individual, a brand-new product of personal inspiration, a creation with no relations to works of the past. Second, we must understand that a text is not only the product of a pre-existing combinatorial system (constituted by all that is literature *in posse*); it is also a transformation of that system.

We can already say, then, that every literary study must participate in a double movement: from the particular work to literature generally (or genre), and from literature generally (from genre) to the particular work.

SOURCE: Todorov, T. (1973). *The Fantastic: A Structural Approach to a Literary Genre* (R. Howard, Trans.). Press of Case Western Reserve University.

12

Conclusions

The Figure and the Ground

The relationship between individual works (novels, films, TV shows) and genres (detective, science fiction, spy, etc.) strikes me as being a figure-ground one. Texts have an integrity of their own and are "wholes" that stand on their own two feet (so to speak), but they also have meaning relative to something broader, the genre which they can be subsumed under (or, in some cases, the genres, in that mixed-genre texts are possible).

This book is written in a period of time when literary theory seems to be the rage in academia and novels, films, and television shows only have relevance, it is suggested, as grist for the critic's mill. Critics now seem to feel that they are more important than creators, whose basic function it is to provide texts for the critics to analyze and about which they can elaborate, spin, and evolve theories of literature, communication, and so on. The world, in short, has been turned upside down. How long this state of affairs will last remains to be seen.

This situation (to the extent I am correct, and I confess to exaggerating and overgen(re)eralizing a bit to make a point) probably developed because, for so long, we assumed that texts were understood, intuitively, by everyone, more or less the same way.

Elevating literary and communications theory also has the tendency to make glad the hearts of critics and theorists who, until recently, labored in the shadows. We have always had criticism. A great deal of what goes on in English departments, humanities departments, film departments, theatre departments, communications departments, art departments is criticism—and that has been the case for decades. Criticism is, after all, infinitely more interesting and entertaining than teaching composition.

What I am talking about is the enthusiasm and ardor with which literary theory and related concerns (media criticism, communication theory, etc.) are now carried on, as if it were something of awesome importance in the scheme of things. Maybe it is? And I, I must confess, am in league with those who carry the flag for literary and media theory. Another reason that theory has become so important is that it has leaped beyond the confines of literature and the arts and has metamorphasized, like Kafka's Gregor Samsa, into culture criticism, and, in particular, social and political criticism.

This is where genres come in. They are more than simple classificatory schemas for categorizing texts; they have, we see, in many cases, social and political significance. It is hard to define and characterize the notion of genre with precision. There is something slippery about the concept. In addition, certain genres, such as science fiction, are very hard to deal with. Where does one draw the line between, say, science fiction and horror? I have suggested that horror is a separate genre, but many would disagree with me.

The Design of the Book

In this book I have done two things. First, I have dealt with genres from a theoretical perspective, and have tried to suggest how they are structures, how they relate to narratives and to formulas as well as to society and culture. Second, I have taken texts that I consider to be representative or classic examples from the more important genres and analyzed these texts. I wanted to avoid the survey, once-over-quickly kind of chapter one sometimes finds in books on genres, in which a major genre, such as the detective story, is dealt with in 20 or 30 pages, if that. These survey chapters have their uses, but I also think it is good to examine an important text in some detail. I focused on the figure, one might say, and not the ground.

I have neglected, of course, many important genres from a variety of media. I have not written anything on situation comedies, domestic comedies, quiz programs, news shows, sports shows—the list could go on and on. But I have provided, in the first section of this book, methodologies and perspectives that others can use to deal with any genres that interest them. I have also dealt with many of these genres in an earlier book, *The TV-Guided American* (Berger, 1976). Although *The TV-Guided American* is not explicitly about genres, the book actually deals with significant shows from most of the important television genres.

There is a good deal that remains to be done, of course. Genre theory still remains elusive, and demands attention. So do the various genres. There are a number of books in this area, fortunately, but we can still use more. And finally, of course, individual texts need to be interpreted, related to their genres and to society and culture, in general.

I would hope that this little book will stimulate interest in the nature of genres and in genre criticism and will help those who are involved in "reading" texts to do so in more perceptive and useful ways. If you have obtained some ideas from this book that have affected the way you analyze and interpret texts, its purpose will have been served.

References

Allen, D. (1971). *Science fiction: The future.* New York: Harcourt Brace Jovanovich.
Aristotle. (1941). *The basic works of Aristotle* (R. McKeon Ed. and Trans.). New York: Random House.
Ash, B. (Ed.). (1977). *The visual encyclopedia of science fiction.* New York: Harmony House.
Bakhtin, M. M. (1981). *The dialogic imagination.* Austin, TX: University of Texas Press.
Bennett, T., & Woollacott, J. (1987). *Bond and beyond: The political career of a popular hero.* London: Methuen.
Berger, A. A. (1976). *The TV-guided American.* New York: Walker.
Berger, A. A. (1990). *Agitpop: Political culture and communication theory.* New Brunswick, NJ: Transaction.
Berger, A. A. (Ed.). (1991). *Media USA* (2d ed., 1st ed. 1988). White Plains, NY: Longman.
Bettelheim, B. (1975). *The uses of enchantment: The meaning and importance of fairy tales.* New York: Knopf.
Brenner, C. (1974). *An elementary textbook of psychoanalysis.* New York: Anchor.
Bywater, T., & Sobchack, T. (1989). *Introduction to film criticism: Major critical approaches to narrative film.* White Plains, NY: Longman.
Cantril, H. (1966). *The invasion from Mars: A study in the psychology of panic.* New York: Harper Torchbooks.
Cawelti, J. (1971). *The six-gun mystique.* Bowling Green, OH: Bowling Green University Popular Press.
Christie, A. (1940). *Murder on the Orient Express.* New York: Pocket Books.
Clareson, T. D. (Ed.). (1971). *SF: The other side of Realism: Essays on modern fantasy and science fiction.* Bowling Green, OH: Bowling Green University Popular Press.
Culler, J. (1975). *Structuralist poetics: Structuralism, linguistics, and the study of literature.* Ithaca, NY: Cornell University Press.
Denney, R. (1989). *The astonished muse.* New Brunswick, NJ: Transaction.
Dichter, E. (1960). *The strategy of desire.* London: Boardman.

160

References   161

Douglas, M., & Wildavsky, A. (1982). *Risk and culture.* Berkeley: University of California Press.

Eagleton, T. (1983). *Literary theory: An introduction.* Minneapolis: University of Minnesota Press.

Eco, U. (1985, Fall). Innovation and repetition: Between modern and post-modern aesthetics. *Daedalus.*

Esslin, M. (1982). *The age of television.* San Francisco, CA: W. H. Freeman.

Fleming, I. (1958). *Dr. No.* New York: Signet.

Frye, N. (1957). *Anatomy of criticism.* Princeton, NJ: Princeton University Press.

Gowans, A. (1981). *Learning to see: Historical perspectives on modern popular/commercial arts.* Bowling Green, OH: Bowling Green University Popular Press.

Grotjahn, M. (1966). *Beyond laughter: Humor and the subconscious.* New York: McGraw-Hill.

Hammett, D. (1972). *The Maltese Falcon.* New York: Vintage.

Heuscher, J., Jr. (1974). *A psychiatric study of myths and fairy tales.* Springfield, IL: Charles C Thomas.

Hollister, B. (Ed.). (1974). *Another tomorrow: A science fiction anthology.* Dayton, OH: Pflaum.

Kakutani, M. H. (1980, September 7). Exotic packaged romance: Always and forever. *This World*, magazine, *San Francisco Chronicle.*

Kaminsky, S. M. (1974). *American film genres: Approaches to a critical theory of popular film.* Dayton, OH: Pflaum.

Kaminsky, S. M., & Mahan, J. H. (1986). *American television genres.* Chicago, IL: Nelson-Hall.

Kellner, D. (1980). Television images, codes and messages. *Televisions,* 7(4), 74.

Kitses, J. (1970). *Horizons west.* Bloomington: Indiana University Press.

Lehr, J. (1988, January/February). Me Tarzan, you, Odysseus: Classical myth in popular culture. *Iowa Alumni Review.*

Lévi-Strauss, C. (1967). *Structural anthropology.* New York: Anchor.

Lodge, D. (Ed.). (1988). *Modern criticism and theory: A reader.* White Plains, NY: Longman.

Lotman, Y. (1977). *The structure of the artistic text* (Gail Lenhoff & Ronald Vroon Trans.). Ann Arbor: Michigan Slavic Contributions, no. 7.

Lowndes, R. A. W. (1970). The contributions of Edgar Allen Poe. In F. M. J. Nevins (Ed.), *The mystery writer's art.* Bowling Green, OH: Bowling Green University Popular Press.

Mays, M. (1971). *Frankenstein*: Mary Shelley's Black Theodicy. In T. D. Clareson (Ed.), *SF: The other side of realism: Essays on modern fantasy and science fiction.* Bowling Green, OH: Bowling Green University Popular Press.

Nelson, J. (1988). TV-formulas: Prime-time glue. In A. A. Berger (Ed.), *Media USA* (1st ed.). White Plains, NY: Longman. (Article originally published in *In Search,* 1979.)

Nevins, F. M. J. (Ed.). (1970). *The mystery writer's art.* Bowling Green, OH: Bowling Green University Popular Press.

O'Connor, J. J. (1990, October 4). Black sitcoms steeped in high concept. *New York Times.*

Propp, V. (1968). *Morphology of the folktale* (Introduction by Alan Dundes) (2d ed.). Austin, TX: University of Texas Press. (Originally published in 1928.)

Randall, J. H., Jr., & Buchler, J. (1962). *Philosophy: An introduction*. New York: Barnes and Noble.

Roloe, C. J. (1957). *Simeon and Spillane: The metaphysics of murder for the millions*. In B. Rosenberg & D. M. White, *Mass culture: The popular arts in America*. New York: Free Press.

Rosenberg, B. (1986). *Genreflecting: A guide to reading interests in genre fiction*. Littleton, CO: Libraries Unlimited.

Rosenberg, B., & White, D. M. (1957). *Mass culture: The popular arts in America*. New York: Free Press.

Saussure, F. de (1966). *Course in general linguistics*. New York: McGraw-Hill.

Scholes, R. (1974). *Structuralism in literature*. New Haven, CT: Yale University Press.

Shelley, M. (1967). *Frankenstein or the modern Prometheus*. New York: Bantam Pathfinder Editions.

Sontag, S. (1965). The imagination of disaster. In D. Allen, *Science fiction: The future*. New York: Harcourt Brace Jovanovich

Steiner, G. (1991). Radio: What once made it ours and ours alone. In A. A. Berger (Ed.), *Media USA* (2d ed.). White Plains, NY: Longman.

Thompson, M., Ellis, R., & Wildavsky, A. (1990). *Cultural theory*. Boulder, CO: Westview Press.

Todorov, T. (1973). *The fantastic: A structural approach to a literary genre* (R. Howard Trans.). Cleveland, OH: Press of Case Western Reserve University.

Todorov, T. (1988). The topology of detective fiction. In D. Lodge (Ed.), *Modern criticism and theory: A reader*. White Plains, NY: Longman.

Turner, G. (1977). Science fiction as literature. In B. Ash (Ed.), *The visual encyclopedia of science fiction*. New York: Harmony House.

Vande Berg, L., & Wenner, L. A. (Eds.). (1991). *Television criticism: Approaches and applications*. White Plains, NY: Longman.

Warshow, R. (1964). *The immediate experience*. New York: Anchor.

Wells, H. G. (1964). *War of the Worlds*. New York: Airmont Publishing.

Wildavsky, A. (1986). Choosing preferences by constructing institutions: A cultural theory of preference formation. Presidential address, American Political Science Association. Reprinted in A. A. Berger (Ed.) (1989). *Political culture and public opinion*. New Brunswick, NJ: Transaction.

Wright, W. (1975). *Six-guns and society*. Berkeley: University of California Press.

Name Index

163

Subject Index

About the Author

Arthur Asa Berger is Professor of Broadcast Communication Arts at San Francisco State University, where he has taught since 1965. He has written extensively on popular culture, the mass media, and related concerns. Among his books are *Media Analysis Techniques, Agitpop: Political Culture and Communication Theory, Seeing Is Believing,* and *Media USA.*

Berger had a Fulbright to Italy in 1963 and taught at the University of Milan. He has lectured extensively on media and popular culture—in Denmark, Norway, Sweden, and Finland as a guest of the Nordic Institute of Folklore; in Greece, Lebanon, and Turkey in 1973 and in Brazil in 1987 for the United States Information Agency; and in Germany, France, the People's Republic of China, and England at the request of various universities and institutions. He is a film and television review editor for *Society* magazine, editor of a series of reprints, "Classics in Communications" for Transaction Books, and a consulting editor for *Humor* magazine. He has appeared on *20/20* and the *Today* show, and appears frequently on various local television and radio stations in the San Francisco area. *Popular Culture Genres* is Berger's twentieth book and fourth book for Sage Publications.

Printed in the United Kingdom
by Lightning Source UK Ltd.
101635UKS00001BA/130-138